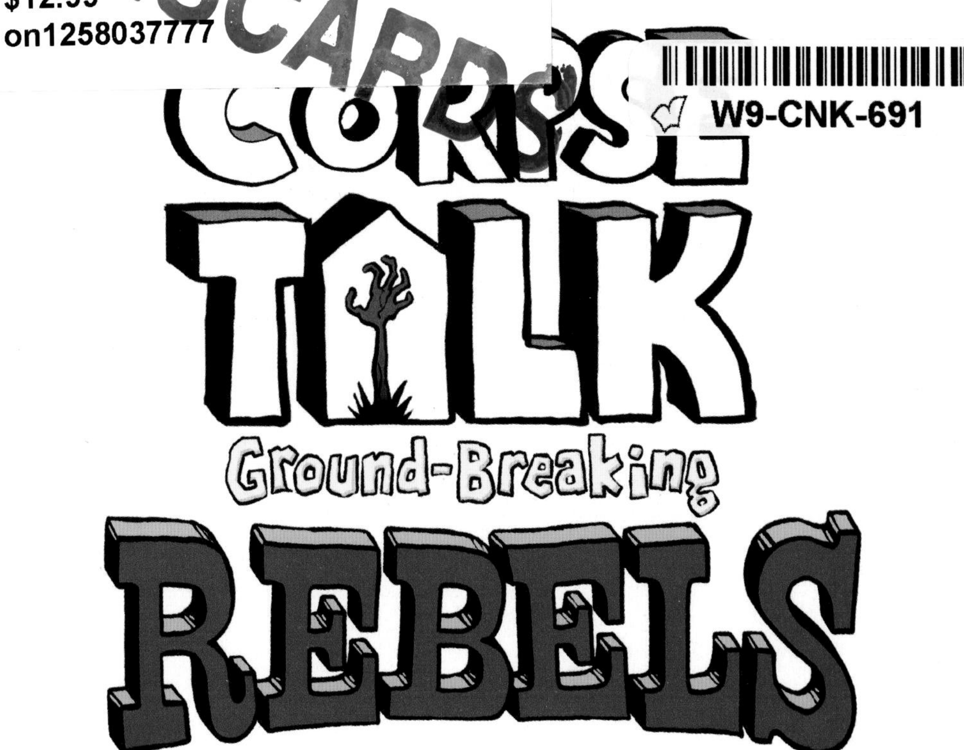
CORPSE
TALK
Ground-Breaking
REBELS

DK

Te vas? No.
COMPLETE ARMOR LATE XVI CENTURY
COMPLETE ARMOR XVI CENTURY
1675 LATE ARMOR
THREE QUARTER SUIT
1580
1515
GOTHIC
1460
1440 GOTHIC
POST ROMAN
650
850 FRANKISH
1050 NORMAN
CHAIN MAIL
1350 TRANSITIONAL MAIL AND PLATE
WOMEN'S SUFFRAGE
MARCH and MASS-MEETING
SATURDAY JUNE 13th
EMBANKMENT 3.
ALBERT HALL 4.30
ALAS ROTAS
VOTES FOR WOMEN

We the People
Article. I.
CORPSE TALK
Ground-Breaking
REBELS
God is Truth
The way to Truth
lies through ahimsa
(non violence)
sabarmati
13, 3, 27
mkgandhi

HELLO, EVERYONE AND WELCOME TO CORPSE TALK, THE COMIC-BOOK CHAT SHOW.
WITH ME, YOUR HOST, ADAM MURPHY.
FOR AS LONG AS THERE HAVE BEEN RULERS, THERE HAVE BEEN REBELS.
PEOPLE BRAVE, OR CRAZY, ENOUGH TO STAND UP AND SAY, "YOU'RE NOT THE BOSS OF ME."
BUT WHAT IS IT THAT IGNITES OTHERWISE COMPLIANT CIVILIANS TO TURN INTO FURIOUS FIREBRANDS?
A BURNING HATRED OF OPPRESSION?
AN UNBEARABLE LOATHING OF BEING TOLD WHAT TO DO?
AN UNQUENCHABLE RAGE AT THE MEMORY OF ANCIENT INJUSTICES?
LIKE BEING SENT TO BED WHEN IT WASN'T EVEN DARK OUT!

THESE ARE JUST SOME OF THE HARD-HITTING QUESTIONS I WOULD LOVE TO ASK HISTORY'S RADICAL RENEGADES!
BUT NOW, THANKS TO THE LIMITLESS POSSIBILITIES OF COMICS...
...I CAN!
SO GET READY TO DIG THE DIRT ON SOME OF HISTORY'S MOST ICONIC ICONOCLASTS!
RIGHT HERE ON CORPSE TALK, THE SHOW THAT BRINGS THE DEAD FAMOUS TO LIFE!

CONTENTS

OK, SO, WHAT BETTER WAY TO KICK OFF A BOOK OF REBELS THAN WITH THE MAN WHO **SURMOUNTED SLAVERY** TO STRIKE **TERROR** INTO THE HEART OF THE **ROMAN EMPIRE**.
IT'S THE **REBEL WITHOUT AN ESCAPE CLAUSE**, THE **TOUGH GUY FROM THRACE**...
SPARTACUS!
SPARTACUS
GLADIATOR
111BCE–71BCE

SPARTACUS, YOUR FREEDOM FIGHT AGAINST THE UNDEFEATED MIGHT OF ROME BEGAN IN **GLADIATOR SCHOOL**. WHICH, YOU MUST ADMIT, SOUNDS TOTALLY **AWESOME**...

-SIGH-
OK, LET ME EXPLAIN TO YOU HOW **TOTALLY NOT** AWESOME IT WAS...

GLADIATORS WERE IMPRISONED SLAVES, FORCED TO FIGHT ONE ANOTHER LIKE ANIMALS FOR THE ROMANS' ENTERTAINMENT.

THE "SCHOOL" WAS A PRISON WHERE THEY TRAINED US TO KILL OR BE KILLED, LIKE ANIMALS.

BUT I WAS **NOT** AN ANIMAL. I WAS A **MAN**. SO WHEN THE CHANCE TO ESCAPE CAME, I TOOK IT.

I STARTED A RIOT THAT KILLED OUR JAILERS, AND WE MADE A RUN FOR IT.

ANYONE WANNA SWAP...?

ONCE OUTSIDE, WE FOUND A CART FULL OF GLADIATOR WEAPONS...

THAT'S MORE LIKE IT!

...AND THEN, WHEN A GROUP OF SOLDIERS TRIED TO RECAPTURE US, WE BEAT THEM AND TOOK THEIR WEAPONS, TOO.

AW YEAH!

WE ESCAPED TO NEARBY **MOUNT VESUVIUS**, AN ACTIVE **VOLCANO**.

THERE WAS ONLY **ONE** PATH UP AMID ITS SHEER CLIFFS, SO WHILE WE STAYED THERE, WE WERE SAFE.

BUT THE ROMANS KNEW WE'D HAVE TO COME DOWN FOR FOOD, SO THEY TRIED TO **STARVE** US OUT.

BUT I FOUND ANOTHER WAY. WE CUT DOWN VINES AND MADE ROPE LADDERS...

AND THEN SCALED DOWN THE CLIFFS—KILLING THE ROMANS WHILE THEY SLEPT.

LIKE NINJAS!
I HAVE NO IDEA WHAT THAT IS.

I RAMPAGED UP AND DOWN ITALY, DEFEATING ROMANS, PLUNDERING FARMS AND FREEING SLAVES, TRAINING THEM TO FIGHT BY MY SIDE.

FROM YOUR INITIAL BAND OF JUST **80** GLADIATORS, YOUR ARMY SWELLED TO OVER **100,000**.

AND YOU WON VICTORY AFTER VICTORY AGAINST EVERY ARMY ROME SENT AGAINST YOU.
SLAVES
ROMANS
III

IT SEEMED THAT YOU WERE **INVINCIBLE**!

YES... BUT THAT WAS THE PROBLEM.

MY GUYS STARTED THINKING WE REALLY **WERE** INVINCIBLE, SO THEY REFUSED TO ESCAPE ACROSS THE ALPS TO SAFETY.

AND THE ROMANS WERE **SO TERRIFIED** OF US, THEY SENT IN ONE OF THEIR **BEST GENERALS**...

MARCUS **CRASSUS**, A MAN SO RUTHLESS THAT HIS **OWN MEN** WERE AFRAID OF HIM.

IF THEY LOST A BATTLE OR RAN AWAY, HE HAD THEM **DECIMATED**.
RANDOM **1** IN EVERY **10** SOLDIERS EXECUTED.

WITH HIS MEN INSPIRED BY **FEAR**, CRASSUS STARTED WINNING BATTLES, AND WE STARTED LOSING.
SLAVES
ROMANS
V
IV

I TRIED TO ARRANGE FOR SOME PIRATES TO SHIP US OUT OF ITALY, PAYING THEM WITH TREASURE WE'D PLUNDERED FROM THE ROMANS' FARMS.

BUT THEY BETRAYED US, TOOK THE MONEY, AND JUST SAILED AWAY...
OH, COME ON. HOW DID YOU NOT SEE THAT COMING!?

WITH NO WAY OUT AND MASSIVE ROMAN REINFORCEMENTS EXPECTED ANY DAY, THERE WAS NOTHING LEFT TO DO BUT A FINAL DESPERATE BATTLE.

I TRIED TO FIGHT MY WAY TO CRASSUS.
YOU'RE GOIN' DOWN!
YEAH? TRY IT!

BUT IN THE END, I GOT SURROUNDED, SEPARATED FROM MY MEN, AND SPEARED THROUGH THE LEG.

I FOUGHT ON TO THE END, BUT IT WAS HOPELESS...

YOUR REBELLION WAS BRUTALLY SUPRESSED, WITH MOST OF THE SLAVES BEING SLAUGHTERED ON THE BATTLEFIELD.

AND THE 5,000 SURVIVORS ROUNDED UP AND CRUCIFIED.
SO DON'T GET ANY IDEAS!
YES, BOSS.

BUT ALTHOUGH THE REBELLION FAILED, IN ANOTHER WAY, YOU SUCCEEDED. YOUR UNBREAKABLE DETERMINATION TO WIN FREEDOM AT ANY COST HAS BEEN AN INSPIRATION THROUGHOUT THE AGES.

SO THAT, WHEREVER PEOPLE SUFFER UNDER THE OPPRESSION OF TYRANNY, THEY CAN DRAW ON YOUR EXAMPLE, TO STAND TALL AND SAY WITH PRIDE...

"I AM SPARTACUS!"
YEAH. I'D STILL RATHER HAVE SURVIVED...

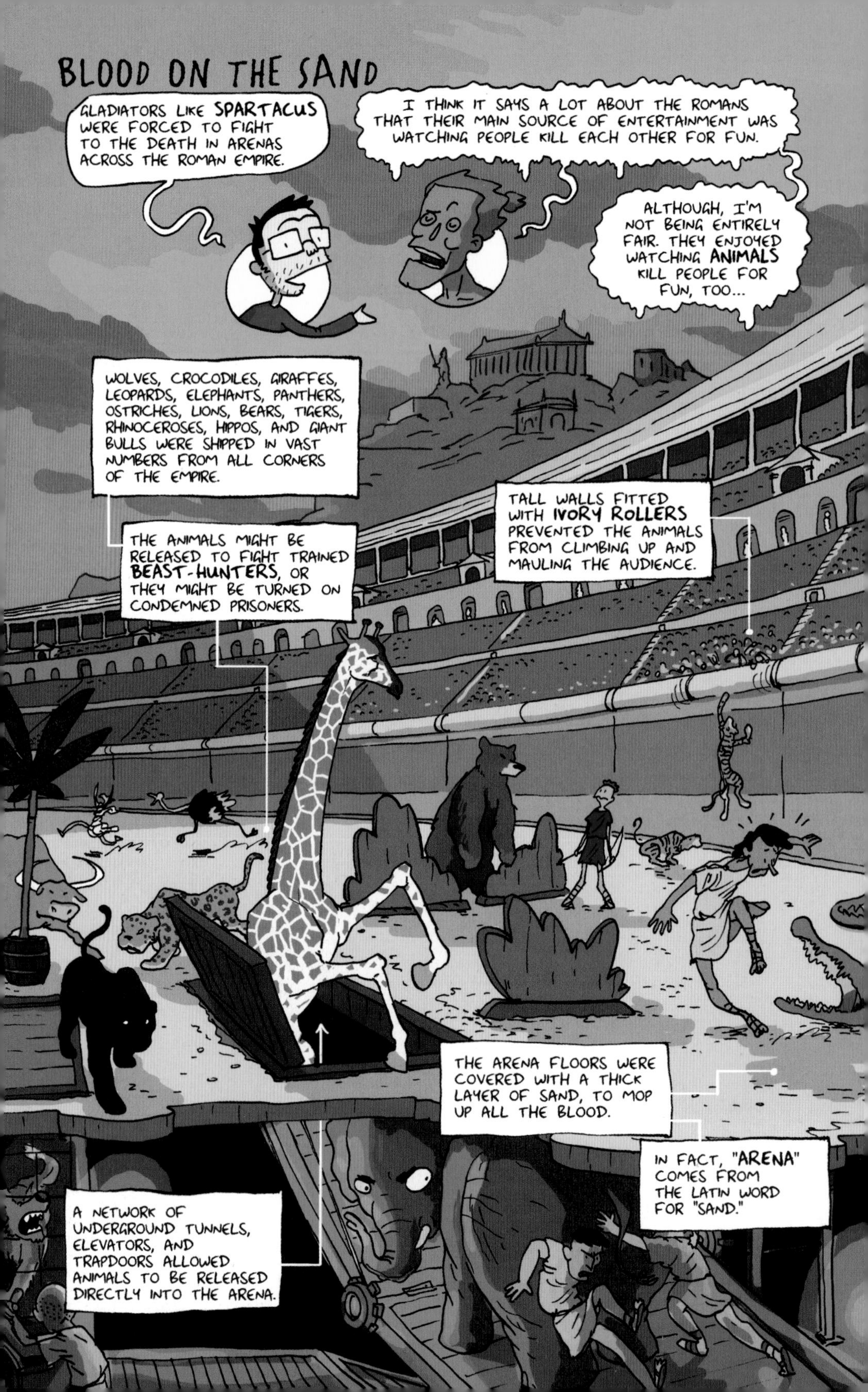
BLOOD ON THE SAND
GLADIATORS LIKE SPARTACUS WERE FORCED TO FIGHT TO THE DEATH IN ARENAS ACROSS THE ROMAN EMPIRE.
I THINK IT SAYS A LOT ABOUT THE ROMANS THAT THEIR MAIN SOURCE OF ENTERTAINMENT WAS WATCHING PEOPLE KILL EACH OTHER FOR FUN.
ALTHOUGH, I'M NOT BEING ENTIRELY FAIR. THEY ENJOYED WATCHING ANIMALS KILL PEOPLE FOR FUN, TOO...
WOLVES, CROCODILES, GIRAFFES, LEOPARDS, ELEPHANTS, PANTHERS, OSTRICHES, LIONS, BEARS, TIGERS, RHINOCEROSES, HIPPOS, AND GIANT BULLS WERE SHIPPED IN VAST NUMBERS FROM ALL CORNERS OF THE EMPIRE.
THE ANIMALS MIGHT BE RELEASED TO FIGHT TRAINED BEAST-HUNTERS, OR THEY MIGHT BE TURNED ON CONDEMNED PRISONERS.
TALL WALLS FITTED WITH IVORY ROLLERS PREVENTED THE ANIMALS FROM CLIMBING UP AND MAULING THE AUDIENCE.
THE ARENA FLOORS WERE COVERED WITH A THICK LAYER OF SAND, TO MOP UP ALL THE BLOOD.
IN FACT, "ARENA" COMES FROM THE LATIN WORD FOR "SAND."
A NETWORK OF UNDERGROUND TUNNELS, ELEVATORS, AND TRAPDOORS ALLOWED ANIMALS TO BE RELEASED DIRECTLY INTO THE ARENA.

AFTER THE BEAST-FIGHTS, CAME THE MAIN EVENT—THE GLADIATORS.
GLADIATORIAL GAMES WERE ORGANIZED AND PAID FOR BY THE SUPER-RICH TO CURRY FAVOR WITH THE PUBLIC, BOTH TO GAIN THEIR SUPPORT IN ELECTIONS AND JUST TO KEEP THEM FROM REVOLTING.
GLADIATORS ENTERED THROUGH THE DOOR OF LIFE, WHICH CONNECTED TO THE GLADIATOR SCHOOL NEXT DOOR.
IF THEY WERE LUCKY THEY LEFT THROUGH THAT DOOR, TOO.
THE UNLUCKY ONES LEFT THROUGH THE DOOR OF DEATH.
BEFORE DELIVERING THE FINAL BLOW, THE VICTOR HAD TO CHECK WITH THE EDITOR (THE OFFICIAL IN CHARGE: USUALLY THE GUY WHO'D PAID FOR THE WHOLE THING).
THERE WERE DIFFERENT TYPES OF GLADIATORS, AND THEY ALL HAD DIFFERENT WEAPONS, ARMOR, AND FIGHTING STYLES.
SPARTACUS FOUGHT AS A MURMILLO, A SLOW, HEAVILY ARMORED CLASS, OFTEN PITTED AGAINST THE RETARIUS, A FAST, LIGHTLY ARMORED FIGHTER.
IF HE HAD FOUGHT HONORABLY, THE LOSER MIGHT BE SPARED.
THIS WAS SIGNALED BY HIDING THE THUMB INSIDE THE FIST.
BUT IF HE HAD FOUGHT POORLY, RUN AWAY, OR EVEN JUST IF THE CROWD WERE IN A BAD MOOD, HE GOT THE "TURNED THUMB" (LIKELY A STABBING MOTION).
SO NOT QUITE THE MODERN THUMBS UP AND DOWN, BUT CLOSE...
I GIVE THE WHOLE THING A BIG THUMBS TURNED.

NEXT UP IS ONE OF THE MOST LEGENDARY **LEADING LADIES** OF THE ANCIENT WORLD, THE **BATTLE-HARDENED BOSS** OF THE **BATTLING BRITONS**.
SHE'S THE **WARRIOR QUEEN** OF THE **INDOMITABLE ICENI**, IT'S...
BOUDICCA!
BOUDICCA
ICENI QUEEN
c.30–61

BOUDICCA, YOU HAD SOME **SERIOUS BEEF** WITH THE ANCIENT ROMANS! WHAT WAS ALL **THAT** ABOUT?

WELL, WHEN THEY FIRST ARRIVED HERE IN BRITAIN, WE THOUGHT THEY WERE ALL RIGHT! AND THEY BROUGHT PEACE AND PROSPERITY.

MY HUSBAND, **KING PRASUTAGUS**, MADE A DEAL WHERE WE WOULD REMAIN AN INDEPENDENT KINGDOM.

ROMANS
ICENI

BUT WHEN HE DIED, THE ROMANS CHANGED THEIR MINDS...
HA HA! DEAL'S OFF!

THEY TOOK EVERYTHING.
PLEASE! NOT MY DAUGHTERS!
BEAT IT, LADY. WE'RE IN CHARGE, NOW!

AND WHEN I TRIED TO PROTEST, THEY HAD ME WHIPPED!
LET THIS BE A LESSON TO YOU!

OH MY GOSH! THAT'S TERRIBLE!

I DIDN'T HAVE TIME FOR TEARS! IT WAS TIME FOR REVENGE!

I REMINDED MY PEOPLE OF ALL THE INJUSTICES WE'D SUFFERED.

THEN I LET OUT THE HARE I'D BEEN KEEPING IN MY DRESS FOR JUST THIS OCCASION.
THE... WHAT NOW? THE BIG RABBIT THING?

THE HARE WAS THE SACRED ANIMAL OF THE BRITTONIC WAR GODDESS ANDRASTE, AND WE BELIEVED THE PATH OF ITS RUN WOULD PREDICT HER FAVOR IN BATTLE.
DEFEAT
VICTORY
AND I PREDICTED WE WERE GOING TO KICK SOME SERIOUS ROMAN BUTT!

FIRST WE MARCHED ON CAMULODUNUM (MODERN COLCHESTER), THE HEAVILY FORTIFIED CAPITAL CITY OF THE ROMANS IN BRITAIN, KILLED EVERYONE INSIDE, AND BURNED THE WHOLE PLACE TO THE GROUND.

WHAT WERE THE, YOU KNOW, ROMAN ARMY DOING ABOUT ALL THIS?

OH, A FEW LEGIONS SHOWED UP, BUT THEY WERE NO MATCH FOR MY MASSIVE FORCE!

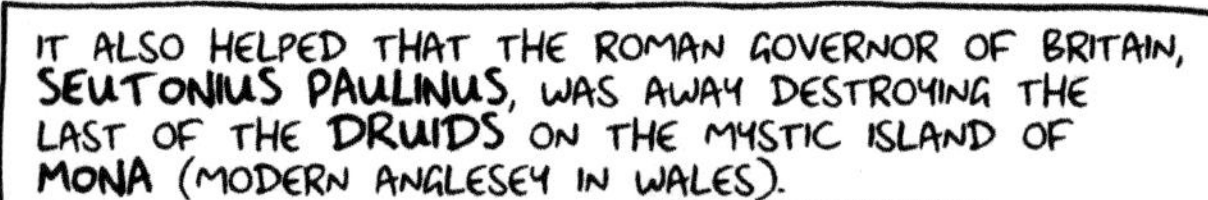

THE ROMANS WERE GENERALLY PRETTY TOLERANT OF LOCAL RELIGIONS, BUT THE DRUIDS, HIGH PRIESTS OF THE CELTIC RELIGION, WERE CONSTANTLY INCITING REBELLIONS.

UH, SIR, I HAVE TO GO TO THE BATHROOM...

ME TOO!

I JUST DID!

DESTROY THIS ONE TINY ARMY, AND WE'D HAVE ENDED THE ROMAN OCCUPATION OF BRITAIN!

AND THEN, WE CHARGED. A TIDAL WAVE OF SCREAMING WARRIORS, HURTLING TOWARD THE ENEMY.

SOME EVEN WENT INTO BATTLE NAKED TO SHOW HOW BRAVE THEY WERE!

BUT THEN, JUST AS WE REACHED THEM...

HEY! NO FAIR!
CLANG!

DEFINITELY NO FAIR!
STAB!

WE HADN'T COUNTED ON THE ROMAN TORTOISE: AN IMPENETRABLE WALL OF SHIELDS, SWORDS AND SPEARS.

WE'D BEEN SO SURE OF VICTORY, WE'D EVEN BROUGHT OUR FAMILIES ALONG TO WATCH...
GO DAD!
WE'RE NUMERAL!!

BIG MISTAKE! AS THE TORTOISE ADVANCED, WE TRIED TO BACK AWAY, AND WERE PINNED AGAINST OUT OWN CARTS.
ARRGH!
GET OUT OF THE WAY!

IT WAS A MASSACRE. EVERYONE WAS SLAUGHTERED.

I COULDN'T LIVE WITH DEFEAT, SO I DRANK POISON!
NOW THAT'S WHAT I CALL A DRAMA QUEEN!

WHAT HAVE THE ROMANS EVER DONE FOR US?
KILLER QUEEN BOUDICCA FAMOUSLY REBELLED AGAINST THE ROMAN OCCUPATION OF BRITAIN.
BUT, A FEW BLOODY INSURRECTIONS ASIDE, THE BRITONS SEEM TO HAVE GENERALLY ACCEPTED THEIR NEW ROMAN OVERLORDS WITH OPEN ARMS.
HMM. I SUPPOSE THAT'S TRUE...
WELL, LET'S HAVE A LOOK AT SOME OF THE BENEFITS OF ROME...
EVERYONE KNOWS ABOUT THE ROMAN ROADS!
10,000 MILES OF STRAIGHT, WELL-CONSTRUCTED ROADS WERE A HUGE IMPROVEMENT OVER THE BRITONS' DIRT TRACKS.
AND THE IMPROVED TRANSPORTATION, ALONG WITH A COMMON CURRENCY, GAVE BRITISH TRADERS ACCESS TO THE MARKETS OF THE WHOLE EMPIRE.
THE BETTER-OFF INHABITANTS OF THE ORDERLY ROMAN TOWNS ENJOYED UNHEARD-OF LUXURIES LIKE RUNNING WATER, HEATED PUBLIC BATHS, AND EVEN GARBAGE DISPOSAL.
BRITAIN TRADED LEAD, TIN, AND WOOL FOR WINE, OLIVE OIL, POTTERY, GLASSWARE, AND PAPYRUS.
THE ROMANS IMPORTED A VARIETY OF NEW FOODS NEVER BEFORE SEEN IN BRITAIN, INCLUDING LEEKS, GARLIC, PEAS, CARROTS, APPLES, AND PEARS.
THEY ALSO BROUGHT THE FIRST CATS TO BRITAIN AS LEGIONARY MASCOTS (CATS WERE CONSIDERED LUCKY BY THE ROMAN ARMY).

BEFORE THE ROMANS ARRIVED, THE BRITISH TRIBES FOUGHT CONSTANTLY, MAKING BRITAIN QUITE A VIOLENT PLACE.
THE ROMAN ARMY IMPOSED THE PAX ROMANA (ROMAN PEACE), BANNED INTER-TRIBAL WARFARE, AND FORCED EVERYONE TO OBEY THE ROMAN LAWS.
AND OF COURSE, HADRIAN'S WALL HELPED KEEP OUT THE TROUBLESOME NEIGHBORS TO THE NORTH.
MAKING ROMAN BRITAIN A MUCH SAFER PLACE FOR EVERYONE.
AND THE LIFESTYLE OF THE BRITONS (OR AT LEAST, THE RICH ELITES) CHANGED COMPLETELY: THEY LEARNED LATIN, BUILT VILLAS, AND EVEN STARTED WEARING TOGAS...
THEY CONTINUED WORSHIPPING THEIR OWN LOCAL GODS (EXCEPT RENAMED TO MATCH THE ROMAN ONES), BUT OTHER RELIGIONS FROM ACROSS THE EMPIRE ALSO BECAME POPULAR.
THE BRITONS EVEN GOT INTO GLADIATOR FIGHTS, CONSTRUCTING AMPHITHEATERS AND BRINGING IN SLAVES TO FIGHT FOR THEIR AMUSEMENT.
OK, SURE, ALL THAT LOOKS SWELL, BUT THE BRITONS WERE STILL A CONQUERED PEOPLE.
IN RETURN FOR ALL THAT ORDER AND PROSPERITY, WE HAD OUR FREEDOM TAKEN BY FORCE.
WAS IT WORTH IT? I DON'T KNOW.
IT CERTAINLY WASN'T FOR ME...

MY NEXT GUEST WAS A **CONSCIENTIOUS CRITIC OF THE CROWN** WHO WENT FROM **BESTIES** TO **WORSTIES** WITH ENGLISH KING **HENRY II**!
PLEASE WELCOME THE MOST POPULAR **MIRACLE-WORKING MARTYR** OF MEDIEVAL ENGLAND...
SAINT THOMAS BECKET!
THOMAS BECKET
SAINT
1118–1170

ST. THOMAS, AFTER YOUR DEATH, THOUSANDS MADE THE PILGRIMAGE TO YOUR SHRINE IN CANTERBURY, ENGLAND EVERY YEAR. BUT YOU DIDN'T START OUT AS A LIKELY CANDIDATE FOR SAINTLY SUPER-STARDOM...

NO, ALAS, I BEGAN MY LIFE AS A POOR MISERABLE SINNER JUST LIKE THE REST OF YOU...

GEE, THANKS.

NOT POOR IN THE **LITERAL** SENSE, YOU UNDERSTAND. AS **CHANCELLOR**, I WAS THE RICHEST AND MOST POWERFUL MAN IN THE REALM, AFTER THE KING OF COURSE.

HENRY AND I WERE THE BEST OF FRIENDS. WE LIVED, WORKED, AND WENT EVERYWHERE TOGETHER.

WE WERE BOTH DRIVEN TO BE THE **BEST**.

AS CHANCELLOR THAT MOSTLY MEANT TAKING PEOPLE'S MONEY.

AND, OF COURSE, CRUSHING THE KING'S ENEMIES, BURNING THEIR HOMES, AND STRIPPING THEM OF ALL THEIR POSSESSIONS.

SO WHEN THE HEAD OF THE ENGLISH CHURCH, THE ARCHBISHOP OF CANTERBURY, DIED, AND HENRY NOMINATED ME TO TAKE OVER, THERE WAS UPROAR.
NOT THAT GUY!
HE'S A GREEDY KILLER, NOT A MAN OF GOD!

HA HA! WITH YOU IN CHARGE, I CAN FINALLY MAKE THE CHURCH DO WHATEVER I WANT!
UH, ABOUT THAT...

HENRY, MY FRIEND, RIGHT NOW I WORK FOR YOU...
AND A FINE JOB YOU'RE DOING!
THANKS.

BUT, IF YOU MAKE ME ARCHBISHOP, I'D BE WORKING FOR GOD. AND SINCE I ALWAYS HAVE TO BE THE BEST, I'LL DO AN EQUALLY GOOD JOB FOR HIM.

I'LL HAVE TO OPPOSE YOU, AND WE'LL BECOME ENEMIES.
PAH! NONSENSE! GREAT BUDDIES LIKE US!? THAT'LL NEVER HAPPEN.

BUT IT DID HAPPEN. YOU BECAME THE ARCHBISHOP AND SUDDENLY YOU WENT FROM EXTRA RICH TO SUPER HOLY.

YOU SWAPPED ALL YOUR RICHES AND FANCY CLOTHES FOR POVERTY, FASTING, AND A HAIR SHIRT. WHAT EVEN IS THAT?

IT'S A SHIRT MADE OF GOAT'S HAIR, WHICH IS BASICALLY THE ITCHIEST SUBSTANCE KNOWN TO MAN.
SWARMING WITH LICE FOR ADDED BITEYNESS.

I WORE IT AS UNDERWEAR, SO IT WOULD **TORMENT** ME CONSTANTLY AS A REMINDER THAT I WAS A **MISERABLE SINNER** WHO DESERVED TO BE PUNISHED.

WOW, THAT'S DEDICATION.
BUT ANYWAY, BACK TO THE STORY.
YOU STARTED OPPOSING HENRY ALL OVER THE PLACE...

HE WANTED TO TAKE OVER THE CHURCH! WELL, THE BEST ARCHBISHOP EVER WASN'T GONNA LET THAT HAPPEN!

DUDE, WHAT IS WRONG WITH YOU!? I'VE GIVEN YOU EVERYTHING, AND NOW YOU'RE OPPOSING ME ALL OVER THE PLACE? WHERE'S THE LOVE!?

MY LOVE IS FOR GOD, WHO HUMBLES THE CRUEL TYRANNY OF KINGS...
DON'T YOU LECTURE ME, PAL!

I'M YOUR KING! YOU HAVE TO DO WHAT I SAY!
GOD IS YOUR KING! YOU HAVE TO DO WHAT HE SAYS!

YEAH. THAT DIDN'T GO DOWN TOO WELL...
THE TWO OF YOU KEPT AT EACH OTHER'S THROATS FOR YEARS...

AT ONE POINT YOU WERE GOING TO DAMN THE WHOLE OF ENGLAND TO HELL BY EXCOMMUNICATING THEM, BUT THE POPE TALKED YOU OUT OF IT.

BUT THE FINAL STRAW CAME WHEN YOU EXCOMMUNICATED SOME BISHOPS WHO HAD TAKEN HENRY'S SIDE...

HENRY WENT BALLISTIC!
WILL NO ONE RID ME OF THIS TURBULENT PRIEST!?*
* ACTUAL QUOTE

HE LATER CLAIMED HE WAS JUST SPOUTING OFF, BUT FOUR OF HIS KNIGHTS TOOK HIM LITERALLY.

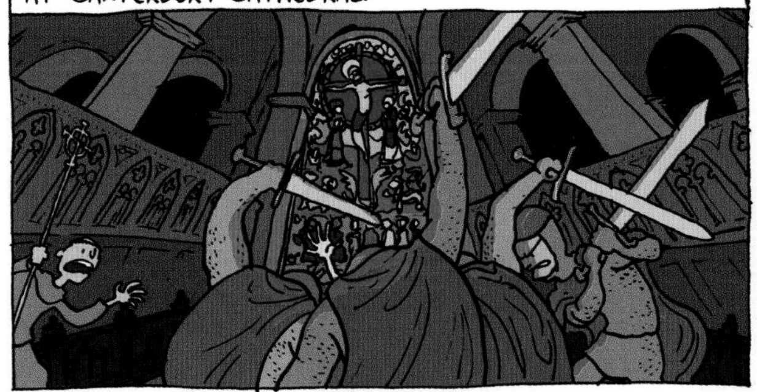

KILLING A PRIEST IN HIS CHURCH WAS AN **UNPARDONABLE SIN.** SOON THE WHOLE CHRISTIAN WORLD WAS UP IN ARMS.

PILLARS OF THE EARTH

SHORTLY AFTER THE MURDER OF ARCHBISHOP ST. THOMAS BECKET, HIS CATHEDRAL AT CANTERBURY CAUGHT FIRE AND HAD TO BE REBUILT.
WHICH WAS A PERFECT OPPORTUNITY FOR THEM TO REMODEL IT INTO A SUITABLY SPLENDID SHRINE FOR A SUPERB SAINT LIKE ME!
CANTERBURY FOLLOWED THE STANDARD PATTERN OF THE NEW GOTHIC-STYLE CATHEDRALS...
BUT WITH A FEW SPECIAL ST. THOMAS TOUCHES.
THE NAVE IS THE MAIN CENTRAL HALL WHERE THE WORSHIPPERS SIT DURING MASS.
THE TRANSEPT CROSSES THE NAVE, TURNING THE WHOLE BUILDING INTO A MASSIVE CHRISTIAN SYMBOL.
THE TRANSEPT ON THE FAR SIDE IS KNOWN AS THE MARTYRDOM—THAT'S WHERE I GOT THE TOP OF MY HEAD CHOPPED OFF.
UNLIKE TODAY, IN THE MIDDLE AGES IT WOULD HAVE BEEN QUITE NOISY. PEOPLE TALKED, ATE, MET FRIENDS, DID BUSINESS, AND EVEN BROUGHT THEIR DOGS TO CHURCH.
THIS IS EXTREMELY NOT COOL, GUYS...

EVERYTHING BEYOND THE CENTRAL CROSSING IS THE MUCH QUIETER **CHANCEL**—ONLY PRIESTS AND PILGRIMS WERE ALLOWED IN.

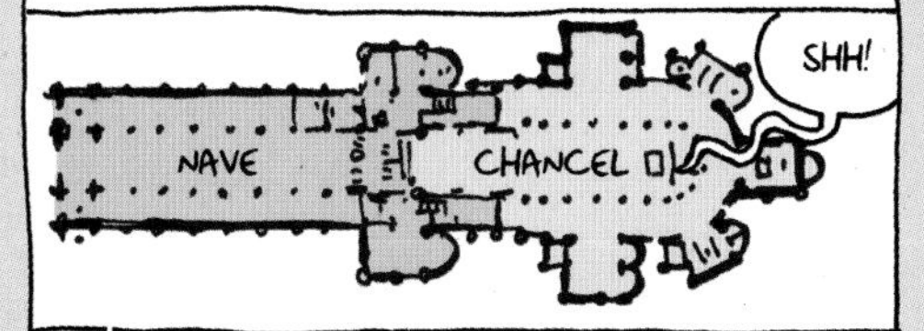

SHH!
NAVE

MASTER MASON **WILLIAM OF SENS** FELL FROM THE ROOF HERE, POOR GUY. INCREDIBLY, HE SURVIVED, BUT HE WAS BADLY WOUNDED AND WAS REPLACED BY HIS APPRENTICE, **WILLIAM THE ENGLISHMAN**.

BE A RIGHT SHAME IF SOMEONE **SLIPPED** UP HERE, EH BOSS?

THE **APSE**, A DOMED CHAPEL, WAS SPECIALLY BUILT TO HOUSE MY AWESOME SHRINE!

PILGRIMS LEFT OFFERINGS OF GOLD, JEWELS, AND **WAX MODELS** OF BODY PARTS THEY WANTED HEALED.

AND AT THE VERY FAR END WAS THE **CORONA**, AN EXTRA TINY CHAPEL WHERE THEY KEPT THE **CHOPPED-OFF TOP OF MY HEAD**—YES, REALLY!

CANTERBURY CATHEDRAL IS STILL THE HOME BASE OF THE **CHURCH OF ENGLAND**. BUT YOU CAN'T ACTUALLY VISIT ST. THOMAS'S SHRINE, SINCE IT WAS DESTROYED BY **HENRY VIII**.
IT WAS **WHAAT!?**
YEAH, WELL, HENRY WASN'T TOO THRILLED ABOUT PEOPLE WHO **DISOBEYED** THEIR **KINGS**.
HE HAD YOU DE-SAINTED AND CARTED OFF ALL THE GOLD AND JEWELS.
HE DIDN'T TAKE THE BODY PARTS THOUGH...

REBEL, TRAITOR, VISIONARY, FREEDOM FIGHTER; MY NEXT GUEST IS A BAD-BOY BARON WHO CAPTURED A KING AND SHOOK UP THE STATUS QUO.
GET READY FOR THE GRANDADDY OF BRITISH AND AMERICAN GOVERNMENT...
SIMON DE MONTFORT!
SIMON DE MONTFORT
REBELLIOUS EARL
1208–1265

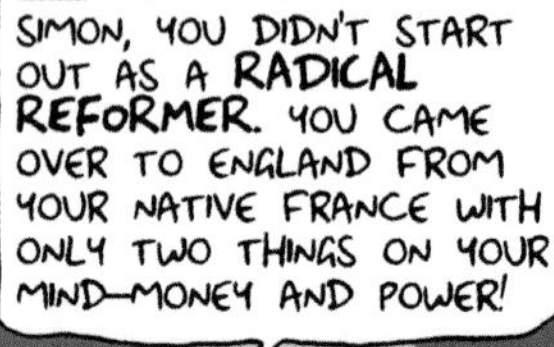
SIMON, YOU DIDN'T START OUT AS A RADICAL REFORMER. YOU CAME OVER TO ENGLAND FROM YOUR NATIVE FRANCE WITH ONLY TWO THINGS ON YOUR MIND—MONEY AND POWER!

YEAH, MY OLDER BROTHER HAD INHERITED ALL THE FAMILY LANDS IN FRANCE, BUT WE HAD SOME LANDS IN ENGLAND TOO, SO I FIGURED WHY NOT TRY MY LUCK THERE?

I SWEET-TALKED THE ENGLISH KING, HENRY III, INTO MAKING ME THE EARL OF LEICESTER.

PLUS I COULDN'T BE SEEN LOOKING SHABBY. AND IT TAKES **CASH MONEY** TO LOOK THIS GOOD!

BUT ALL THOSE JEALOUS LORDS COULDN'T STAND IN THE WAY OF **TRUE LOVE**!
TRUE LOVE!? GET **REAL**!

EARLS CAN'T **AFFORD** TO MARRY FOR **LOVE**—IT'S ALL ABOUT **POWER, STATUS, AND MONEY**!

WELL, YOU HAD PLENTY OF MONEY NOW. CONGRATULATIONS.
YEAH BUT... THE KING AND I HAD AN ARGUMENT...

HOW COME?
HOW **COME!?** BECAUSE HE WAS A BIG **DRIP** WHO COULDN'T HANDLE HAVING **ME** SHOWING HIM UP ALL THE TIME! **THAT'S** HOW COME.

HE STARTED GIVING ALL THE LANDS AND TITLES TO A BUNCH OF **NEW** FAVORITES...

WHICH IS TOTALLY UNFAIR! THE KING SHOULDN'T **HAVE** FAVORITES. HE'S SUPPOSED TO TREAT ALL HIS SUBJECTS EQUALLY!

SO IT WAS OK WHEN **YOU** WERE THE FAVORITE?
THAT IS NOT THE POINT.

A BUNCH OF US LORDS TRIED TO MAKE HIM PROMISE TO DO WHAT WE SAID, BUT HE JUST WENT BACK ON HIS WORD...

I'M APPOINTED BY GOD!
ALSO, HAD MY FINGERS CROSSED!

SO THERE WAS REALLY ONLY ONE THING TO DO: A **HUGE BATTLE** WHERE I CAPTURED THE KING, TOOK HIM PRISONER, AND STARTED RUNNING THINGS MYSELF.

UM... NOW I'M NOT AN EXPERT, BUT ISN'T BEATING UP YOUR KING CONSIDERED **HIGH TREASON?**
NOT IF HE'S A WEAK, CORRUPT DUMMY, **POOP-HEAD** LIKE HENRY III!

BUT YEAH, YOU'RE RIGHT, IT DIDN'T LOOK TOO GOOD. I NEEDED SOME **MAJOR GOODWILL** FROM THE COMMON PEOPLE IF I WAS TO KEEP THEIR SUPPORT.

OOH. HOW'D THE **OTHER** LORDS LIKE THAT IDEA?

YEAH. NOT SO MUCH...

AT THE FINAL BATTLE, I STILL HAD THE KING PRISONER, SO I DRESSED HIM UP IN FULL ARMOR SO NO ONE WOULD RECOGNIZE HIM.

BUT TODAY EVERY DEMOCRATIC COUNTRY IN THE **WORLD** USES A VERSION OF YOUR SYSTEM, WITH REPRESENTATIVES OF **ALL** THE **PEOPLE** MAKING UP THE PARLIAMENT.

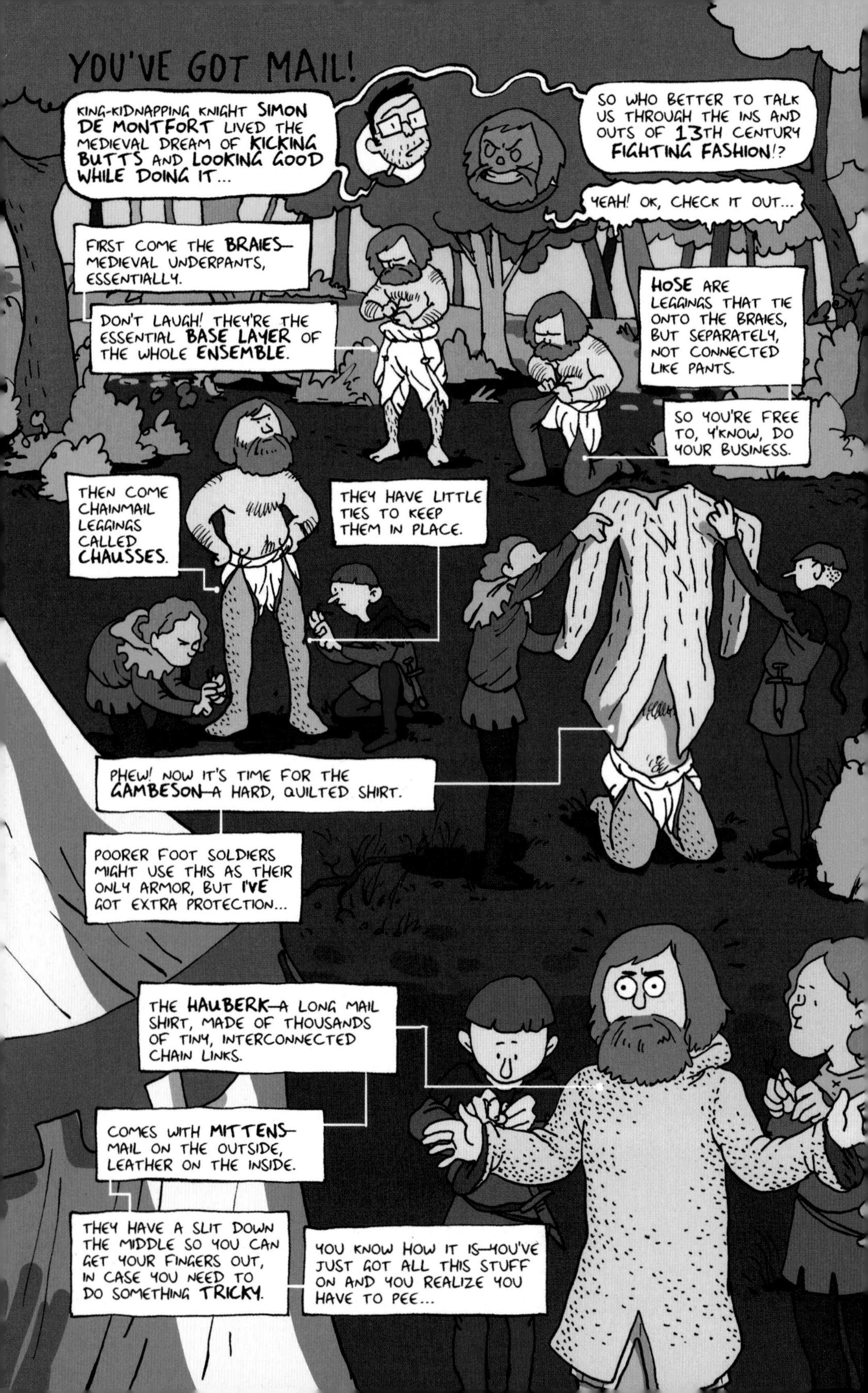
YOU'VE GOT MAIL!
KING-KIDNAPPING KNIGHT SIMON DE MONTFORT LIVED THE MEDIEVAL DREAM OF KICKING BUTTS AND LOOKING GOOD WHILE DOING IT...
SO WHO BETTER TO TALK US THROUGH THE INS AND OUTS OF 13TH CENTURY FIGHTING FASHION!?
YEAH! OK, CHECK IT OUT...
FIRST COME THE BRAIES—MEDIEVAL UNDERPANTS, ESSENTIALLY.
DON'T LAUGH! THEY'RE THE ESSENTIAL BASE LAYER OF THE WHOLE ENSEMBLE.
HOSE ARE LEGGINGS THAT TIE ONTO THE BRAIES, BUT SEPARATELY, NOT CONNECTED LIKE PANTS.
SO YOU'RE FREE TO, Y'KNOW, DO YOUR BUSINESS.
THEN COME CHAINMAIL LEGGINGS CALLED CHAUSSES.
THEY HAVE LITTLE TIES TO KEEP THEM IN PLACE.
PHEW! NOW IT'S TIME FOR THE GAMBESON—A HARD, QUILTED SHIRT.
POORER FOOT SOLDIERS MIGHT USE THIS AS THEIR ONLY ARMOR, BUT I'VE GOT EXTRA PROTECTION...
THE HAUBERK—A LONG MAIL SHIRT, MADE OF THOUSANDS OF TINY, INTERCONNECTED CHAIN LINKS.
COMES WITH MITTENS—MAIL ON THE OUTSIDE, LEATHER ON THE INSIDE.
THEY HAVE A SLIT DOWN THE MIDDLE SO YOU CAN GET YOUR FINGERS OUT, IN CASE YOU NEED TO DO SOMETHING TRICKY.
YOU KNOW HOW IT IS—YOU'VE JUST GOT ALL THIS STUFF ON AND YOU REALIZE YOU HAVE TO PEE...

OK, I'M BACK.
NOW TIE ON A PADDED COIF. IT CUSHIONS YOUR HEAD AND KEEPS YOUR LUSTROUS, FLOWING LOCKS OUT OF YOUR FACE.
THEN YOU CAN PUT ON THE CHAINMAIL HOOD. IT TIES AROUND THE BROW TO KEEP IT FROM SLIPPING.
WE'RE GETTING THERE... NOW THE SURCOAT—A LONG CLOTH WITH YOUR KNIGHTLY COLORS, SO PEOPLE CAN TELL IT'S YOU UNDER ALL THAT GEAR.
SQUIRES WERE A SORT OF APPRENTICE KNIGHT.
ONE OF THEIR MAIN JOBS WAS HELPING THE KNIGHT INTO ALL THIS GEAR—HE CERTAINLY COULDN'T DO IT BY HIMSELF.
LAST COMES THE HEAUME, A PRETTY IMPRESSIVE-LOOKING HELMET.
I'VE GOT THE SWANKY KIND YOU CAN SWING UP AND DOWN, TO GET A BETTER VIEW OF WHAT'S GOING ON.
STRAP ON A SWORD-, AXE, OR MACE-BELT, DEPENDING ON WHAT FORM OF MAYHEM YOU'RE IN THE MOOD FOR THAT DAY...
AND AT LAST, I'M READY TO GO BESTOW SOME BUTT-KICKINGS!

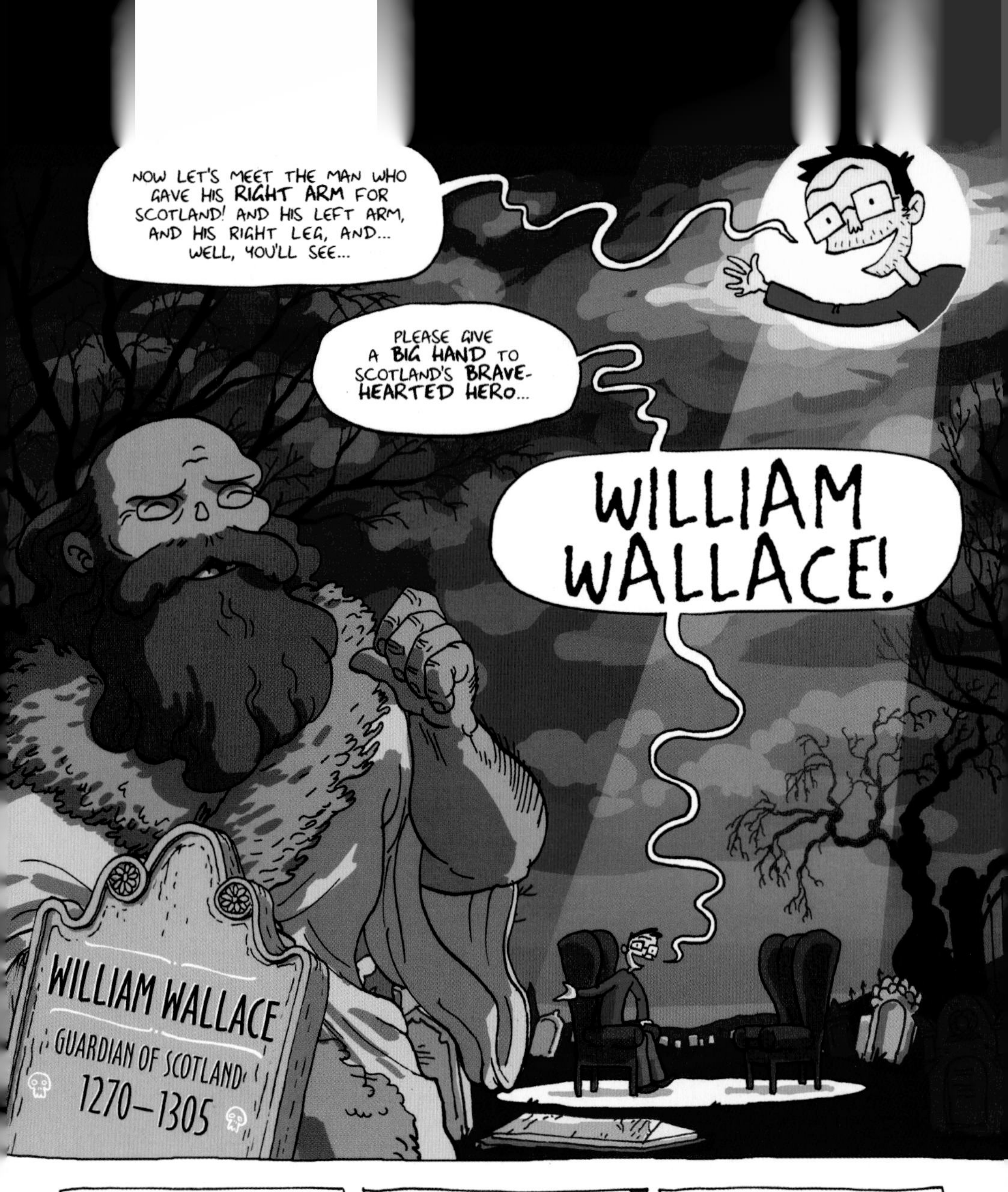
NOW LET'S MEET THE MAN WHO GAVE HIS RIGHT ARM FOR SCOTLAND! AND HIS LEFT ARM, AND HIS RIGHT LEG, AND... WELL, YOU'LL SEE...
PLEASE GIVE A BIG HAND TO SCOTLAND'S BRAVE-HEARTED HERO...
WILLIAM WALLACE!
WILLIAM WALLACE
GUARDIAN OF SCOTLAND
1270–1305

WALLACE, YOU'RE A GREAT HERO TO THE SCOTS FOR DOING WHAT THEY LOVE BEST: BEATING THE ENGLISH! BUT WHY WERE YOU FIGHTING THEM AT ALL?

OCHT. SCOTLAND WAS IN TROUBLE, EVEN BEFORE THE ENGLISH ARRIVED...

FIRST, THE KING FELL OFF A CLIFF, RIDING TO A HOT DATE WITH HIS NEW WIFE.
NOOOOOOOO
NEEEEEEIGH

HE HAD NO CHILDREN, SO THE NEXT IN LINE WAS HIS THREE-YEAR-OLD GRANDDAUGHTER, BUT SHE WAS **DROWNED AT SEA**.
GLUG GLUG...

THE SCOTTISH BARONS STARTED A TUG-OF-WAR OVER WHO SHOULD BE KING...
MY GREAT GRANDUNCLE'S COUSIN WAS KING!
WELL, MY GRANDMOTHER'S FRIEND'S BROTHER WAS KING!
WELL, MY AUNTIE'S CAT'S...

A **CIVIL WAR** WOULD TEAR THE COUNTRY APART! SO SOMEONE HAD A BRIGHT IDEA...
HOLD ON, PEOPLE! LET'S ASK THE ENGLISH KING, **EDWARD I**, TO DECIDE!
OOH, **THAT'S** A GOOD IDEA!

NOPE. **BAD** IDEA! EDWARD CHOSE THE WEAKEST, CRAPPIEST GUY HE COULD FIND...
I CHOOSE **THIS** GUY. I'M **SURE** HE'LL MAKE A GREAT PUPPET—I MEAN, **KING**!
DUUUUR...

SO **HE** COULD CONTROL HIM!
HEY, GUYS! I'VE GOT A GREAT IDEA—LET'S GIVE EDWARD ALL OUR MONEY!
HUH?!
AW WHAT!?

THEN EDWARD SENT IN HIS ARMY, GOT RID OF THE PUPPET, AND MADE **HIMSELF** KING INSTEAD.
WAAAAAH!
HEH HEH.

WELL, I WASN'T GOING TO STAND FOR **THAT**! WE WANTED OUR **OWN** KING, EVEN IF HE **WAS** TERRIBLE!

SO I STARTED AN **UPRISING**! A RAGTAG BAND OF REBELS WITH ONLY ONE GOAL—TO CHASE OUT THE ENGLISH!

BEFORE LONG, YOU WERE EDWARD'S **PUBLIC ENEMY #1**!

WALLACE STOLE ALL MY TAXES!
WALLACE KILLED ALL MY SOLDIERS!
WALLACE **CHOPPED ME IN HALF**!

THIS IS INTOLERABLE! SOMEONE GET UP THERE AND ELIMINATE THIS WALLACE!

SO EDWARD SENT A HUGE ARMY TO KILL YOU AND SUBDUE SCOTLAND!

BUT FIRST HE HAD TO FIND ME! MY SMALLER, LIGHTER ARMY MEANT I COULD WATCH AND WAIT UNTIL THE PERFECT OPPORTUNITY TO ATTACK.

AND THAT OPPORTUNITY CAME WHEN THEY TRIED TO CROSS OVER STIRLING BRIDGE...

THE ENGLISH ARMY WAS BIGGER AND BETTER EQUIPPED, BUT I HAD A PLAN TO TURN THAT AGAINST THEM.

I WAITED UNTIL MOST OF THEM HAD CROSSED THE BRIDGE...

...AND THEN WE ATTACKED!
THE SCOTS!
GET THEM!
GET IN LINE!
GET OUT OF MY WAY!
AAAAAAAAAAAH!
HILL
BRIDGE
MARSHY GROUND

THEIR HEAVILY ARMORED KNIGHTS GOT STUCK IN THE SWAMP, AND THE SCOTS PICKED THEM OFF WITH EXTRA-LONG SPEARS.

THE ENGLISH TRIED TO RETREAT ACROSS THE BRIDGE, WHILE THEIR REINFORCEMENTS TRIED TO CHARGE. IT WAS MAYHEM!
ATTACK!
RETREAT!
GET OFF MY FOOT!

THE BRIDGE COLLAPSED UNDER ALL THEIR WEIGHT, AND THEIR HEAVY ARMOR PULLED THEM DOWN AND DROWNED THEM!

WE WERE ESPECIALLY PLEASED TO HAVE KILLED A GUY CALLED HUGH DE CRESSINGHAM. HE WAS IN CHARGE OF STEALING ALL THE SCOTS' MONEY.
THE JERK!

WE SKINNED HIM AND EVERY SOLDIER GOT A PIECE!
ONE FOR YOU... ONE FOR YOU...
CAN I GET AN EXTRA PIECE? IT'S FOR MY DAUGHTER...

YOU WERE KNIGHTED AND NAMED "HIGH GUARDIAN OF SCOTLAND." YOU WERE RIDING HIGH!
UNTIL I GOT CAPTURED...

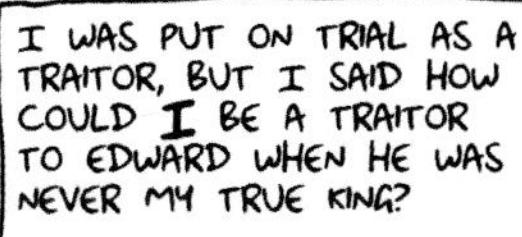
I WAS PUT ON TRIAL AS A TRAITOR, BUT I SAID HOW COULD I BE A TRAITOR TO EDWARD WHEN HE WAS NEVER MY TRUE KING?

I WAS SENTENCED TO BE HANGED, DRAWN, AND QUARTERED! IT WAS THE MOST TORTUROUS MODE OF EXECUTION THEY HAD!

FIRST THEY HANGED ME UNTIL I WAS ALMOST, BUT NOT QUITE, DEAD...

THEN THEY CUT OPEN MY STOMACH, DREW OUT MY GUTS, AND SET THEM ON FIRE.

AND THEN THEY CUT OFF MY HEAD.
AND CUT YOU INTO QUARTERS!
AND CUT ME INTO QUARTERS...

THUMP!

PULL YOURSELF TOGETHER, MAN!

GRIME AND PUNISHMENT
HIRSUTE HARD-MAN WILLIAM WALLACE WAS FAMOUSLY EXECUTED BY BEING HANGED, DRAWN, AND QUARTERED.
BUT THIS WAS JUST ONE OF A MULTITUDE OF MONSTROUS MEDIEVAL PUNISHMENTS.
I THINK THE IDEA WAS THAT THE THREAT OF HORRIFIC TORTURE WOULD TERRIFY PEOPLE INTO BEHAVING.
EXCEPT THE MURDER RATE WAS SOMETHING LIKE 10 TIMES WHAT IT IS TODAY.
SO YEAH...
SO MUCH FOR THAT IDEA.
DEPENDING ON THE SEVERITY OF THE CRIME, THEFT COULD BE PUNISHED WITH FORCED LABOR, FINES, HAVING YOUR HAND CUT OFF, OR THE GIBBET.
PRISONERS WERE STARVED TO DEATH AND THEN LEFT HANGING AS A CONSTANT WARNING.
MURDER WAS PUNISHED BY HANGING.
OR BEHEADING, WHICH WAS A LUXURY RESERVED FOR THE NOBILITY— SO MUCH QUICKER.
UM, HELLO? I'M ACTUALLY AN EARL...
YEAH, YEAH. AN' I'M THE KING'S FAIRY GODMOTHER...
SWINDLING, PUBLIC DRUNKENNESS, AND EVEN VAGRANCY (BEING HOMELESS) WERE ALL CRIMES PUNISHABLE WITH THE STOCKS OR PILLORY.
STOCKS.
PILLORY.
CHEER UP! AT LEAST THEY HAVEN'T DISCOVERED THE PINEAPPLE YET!

HERESY, THAT IS, NOT BELIEVING EXACTLY WHAT THE CHURCH TAUGHT, WAS PUNISHED BY BEING BURNED AT THE STAKE.
THIS WAS ACTUALLY DOING THE HERETIC A FAVOR, SINCE THE FLAMES WOULD PURIFY THEM, SAVING THEM FROM HELL.
IT'S FOR YOUR OWN GOOD, REALLY...
WANNA SWAP THEN?
CONTRARY TO POPULAR BELIEF, WITCHCRAFT WASN'T A BIG CRIME IN THE MIDDLE AGES—HUNTING AND BURNING WITCHES REALLY ONLY GOT GOING IN THE LATER RENAISSANCE PERIOD.
EEE HEE HEE HEE!
BUT BEING HANGED, DRAWN, AND QUARTERED WAS RESERVED FOR THE WORST-POSSIBLE CRIME—BETRAYING THE KING.
ALSO KNOWN AS TREASON.
THE HANGING AND DRAWING PARTS WERE SO GRUESOME THAT THE QUARTERING MUST HAVE SEEMED LIKE A BLESSED RELIEF!
ABOUT TIME!
AFTERWARD, EACH QUARTER WAS POSTED ON A SPIKE IN A DIFFERENT CITY AS A WARNING TO ANY OTHER WOULD-BE REBELS.
OOH! I CAN SEE MY HOUSE FROM HERE...
MY QUARTERS GOT SENT TO NEWCASTLE, BERWICK, STIRLING AND PERTH, AND MY HEAD WAS MOUNTED ON LONDON BRIDGE.
WHICH IS REALLY 5 QUARTERS. I GUESS "HANGED, DRAWN, AND FIFTHED" DOESN'T HAVE THE SAME RING TO IT...

NOW, LET'S MEET THE MAN WHO LED A DECADE OF DEFIANCE AGAINST THE MIGHT OF ENGLAND. TO THE WELSH, HE'S LIKE KING ARTHUR, ROBIN HOOD, AND WILLIAM WALLACE, ALL ROLLED INTO ONE!
PLEASE WELCOME THE LAST WELSHMAN TO EVER HOLD THE TITLE PRINCE OF WALES, IT'S...
OWAIN GLYNDWR*!
OWAIN GLYNDWR
PRINCE OF WALES
1359–1415

OWAIN, FOR A WELSH FREEDOM FIGHTER, YOU WERE REMARKABLY FRIENDLY WITH THE ENGLISH. YOU WERE RAISED BY AN ENGLISH LORD, MARRIED HIS DAUGHTER, AND EVEN FOUGHT IN THEIR ARMY!

YEAH, I WAS ALWAYS COOL WITH THE ENGLISH. I MEAN, OK, THEY'D INVADED US AND KEPT US OPPRESSED BY BRUTAL FORCE, PUNISHING TAXATION, AND UNFAIR LAWS...

BUT THEY'D NEVER DONE ME ANY HARM...
UNTIL, THAT IS, A NEW KING CAME TO THE THRONE, THE DASTARDLY...
DUN DUN DAA...

*THE STANDARD ENGLISH VERSION OF OWAIN'S NAME IS OWEN GLENDOWER. FOR EXTRA CREDIT YOU CAN TRY THE WELSH PRONUNCIATION, WHICH IS SOMETHING LIKE O-WINE GLIN-DOO-IR.

HENRY IV!
BOO!
HEY! WATCH IT...

AS A LORD, I WAS REQUIRED BY LAW TO GO AND FIGHT FOR THE KING WHEREVER AND WHENEVER HE REQUIRED.

BUT MY NEIGHBOR, WHO WAS ANOTHER TRICKY CHARACTER, DIDN'T PASS ON THE SUMMONS, SO I GOT BRANDED AN OUTLAW.
BUT, BUT...
NO EXCUSES.

IMAGINE! ME, THE DESCENDANT OF THREE OF THE PRINCELY HOUSES OF WALES, HIDING IN THE HILLS LIKE A COMMON BANDIT!

BUT THAT WAS JUST THE SORT OF CRAPPY UNFAIRNESS PEOPLE ALL OVER WALES WERE EXPERIENCING, AND THEY WERE GETTING REALLY SICK OF IT!

A GROUP OF DIE HARD DESPERADOES JOINED ME, AND TOGETHER WE SNUCK INTO THE FORTIFIED TOWN OF RUTHIN.

THEN WE THREW OFF OUR DISGUISES, SLAUGHTERED THE ENGLISH GARRISON, AND BURNED THE PLACE TO THE GROUND!

WELL, AFTER A FEW ATTACKS LIKE THAT, HENRY HAD NO CHOICE BUT TO SEND IN AN ARMY TO CAPTURE YOU.

PFF! GOOD LUCK! I WAS IN MY OWN COUNTRY, SURROUNDED BY FRIENDS, AND WITH A TINY FORCE OF GUERRILLAS. HE COULDN'T EVEN FIND ME!

PLUS, THE WEATHER GOT SO TERRIBLE THAT HE HAD TO TURN BACK.
OK. FINE.

PEOPLE STARTED SAYING I WAS A MAGICIAN, WHO COULD EVEN CONTROL THE WEATHER!
THEY'RE GONE. YOU CAN TURN IT OFF NOW.

WHEN HE COULDN'T FIND ME, HENRY TOOK IT OUT ON THE WELSH PEOPLE, WITH MASSACRES AND EVEN MORE BRUTAL TAXES.

BUT THAT JUST MADE THEM MORE DETERMINED. NOW MEN FLOCKED TO THE CAUSE OF A FREE WELSH KINGDOM, WHERE THEY WOULD BE OPPRESSED ONLY BY OTHER WELSHMEN.

VERY NOBLE. BUT ENGLAND WAS SO MUCH BIGGER THAN WALES, AND THEIR ARMIES WERE SO MUCH BIGGER, TOO! HOW COULD YOU HOPE TO SUCCEED?

WELL, FIRSTLY WITH SUPERIOR TACTICS. LIKE AT ONE BATTLE, I'D BRIBED THE ENEMY ARCHERS, SO IN THE MIDDLE OF THE BATTLE, THEY SUDDENLY CAME OVER TO OUR SIDE!

I CAPTURED THE LEADER OF THAT ARMY, A TOP ENGLISH KNIGHT NAMED SIR EDMUND MORTIMER.
UNHAND ME, VARLETS!

NORMAL PROCEDURE WAS TO RANSOM IMPORTANT CAPTIVES, BUT HENRY WOULDN'T PAY! TURNS OUT HE THOUGHT MORTIMER WAS AFTER HIS THRONE.

WELL, IF HE WASN'T BEFORE, HE WAS NOW! TEAMING UP WITH HENRY'S ENEMIES WAS ANOTHER OF MY GIANT-KILLING STRATEGIES.

I REESTABLISHED WELSH LAWS, HELD A WELSH PARLIAMENT, AND WAS CROWNED PRINCE OF WALES. IT WAS A GOLDEN AGE...

BUT IT'S NOT A HAPPY-ENDING STORY, IS IT, OWAIN?

WELL, TIME WAS NOT ON OUR SIDE. AS THE WAR DRAGGED ON, EVERYONE WAS GETTING MORE AND MORE SICK OF IT.

THE ORDINARY PEOPLE WERE FED UP WITH SOLDIERS, ENGLISH AND WELSH, EATING THEIR FOOD AND DYING ON THEIR DOORSTEPS.

PLUS, HENRY HAD THE BRIGHT IDEA OF OFFERING PARDONS TO EVERYONE WHO HAD FOUGHT AGAINST HIM.

SUDDENLY, GIVING THE WHOLE THING UP AND GOING HOME STARTED TO LOOK VERY TEMPTING TO LOTS OF MY GUYS...

I HAD TO DO SOMETHING, AND QUICK! I TEAMED UP WITH THE FRENCH (THOSE GUYS HATED THE ENGLISH EVEN MORE THAN WE DID), AND TOGETHER WE INVADED THEM!
ENGLAND
WALES

HENRY HAD TO COME AND FIGHT. OUR TWO HUGE ARMIES FACED OFF ACROSS A DEEP VALLEY.
GRR!
GRR!

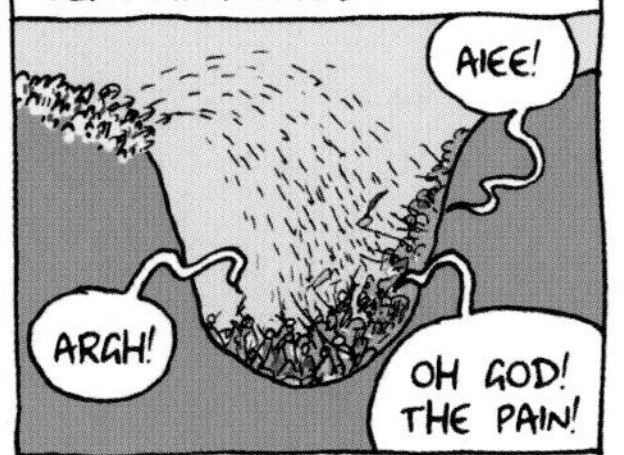
WHICH WAS KIND OF A PROBLEM. IF WE ATTACKED THEM, WE'D HAVE TO GO DOWN INTO THE VALLEY, WHERE WE'D GET SLAUGHTERED.
AIEE!
ARGH!
OH GOD! THE PAIN!

BUT IF THEY ATTACKED US, WE'D DO THE SAME. NO ONE WANTED TO MAKE THE FIRST MOVE!

FOR 8 DAYS WE CAMPED ON THAT HILL, WITH NOTHING TO DO BUT SHARPEN OUR WEAPONS AND WAIT.
I THINK I OVERDID IT...

UNTIL, IN THE END, WE WERE TOO TIRED AND HUNGRY TO FIGHT. HENRY DIDN'T EVEN BOTHER, HE JUST WALKED OFF.
PFF. LATER, LOSERS.

I WANDERED THE HILLS FOR A WHILE, BUT THE HEART HAD GONE OUT OF THE WELSH FIGHT.

AND SO YOUR GREAT CAMPAIGN ENDED, NOT WITH A BANG, BUT WITH A WHIMPER.
NO NEED TO RUB IT IN...

GUERRILLAS IN OUR MIDST

GUERRILLA WARFARE IS THE STRATEGY MOST COMMONLY USED BY MODERN-DAY REBELS FIGHTING AGAINST A LARGER FORCE.
THE WORD WAS FIRST USED BY SPANISH INSURGENTS FIGHTING AGAINST NAPOLEON (IT JUST MEANS "LITTLE WAR" IN SPANISH).
BUT WELSH REBEL LEADER OWAIN GLYNDWR WAS AHEAD OF HIS TIME, USING PROTO-GUERRILLA TACTICS IN HIS WAR AGAINST ENGLISH OCCUPIER HENRY IV HUNDREDS OF YEARS EARLIER!

ALL RIGHT! SO HERE'S OWAIN'S GUERRILLA GUIDELINES, GUARANTEED TO TURN THE TINIEST REVOLT INTO A FULL-ON REVOLUTION!!

AVOID BIG BATTLES.

WITH A SMALLER ARMY, YOU'LL PROBABLY LOSE.

THE ONLY EXCEPTION TO THIS IS IF YOU HAVE SOME SNEAKY TRICKS PLANNED.

LIKE, I DON'T KNOW, ARCHERS HIDING IN THE TREES OR SOMETHING...

KEEP ON THE MOVE.

LESS ARMOR AND FEWER SOLDIERS MEANS YOU CAN TRAVEL FASTER.

HIT THE ENEMY WHEN THEY'RE NOT LOOKING, THEN JUST MELT INTO THE HILLS.

WIN OVER THE PEOPLE WITH CLEVER PROPAGANDA.

LIKE, GET YOUR BARDS TO SING SONGS COMPARING YOU TO THE LEGENDARY KING ARTHUR, ANOTHER GUY WHO BATTLED THE INVADING SAXON HORDES.

YOU COULD ALSO TRY REDUCING TAXES, CHAMPIONING JUSTICE, RESPECTING LOCAL TRADITIONS...

BASICALLY, WHAT IS THE ENEMY DOING THAT EVERYONE'S SICK OF? DO THE OPPOSITE!

CAUSE PROBLEMS.

BURN FARMS AND LOOT TOWNS STILL LOYAL TO THE ENEMY.

YOU'VE GOT NO CHANCE AGAINST A CASTLE, BUT ALL THIS AGGRAVATION WILL HOPEFULLY FORCE THE ENEMY TO COME OUT LOOKING FOR YOU.
THEN YOU CAN POUNCE!
THIS ALSO HELPS WITH THE PROPAGANDA SINCE IT SHOWS THOSE LOCALS THEIR LORDS ARE USELESS AND CAN'T PROTECT THEM.

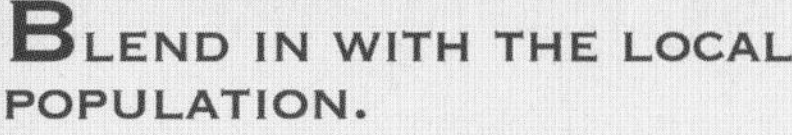

BLEND IN WITH THE LOCAL POPULATION.

EITHER YOU'LL ESCAPE DETECTION, WHICH IS PRETTY SWEET WHEN IT HAPPENS, LET ME TELL YOU...

OR ELSE THE ENEMY WILL ATTACK SOME INNOCENT BYSTANDERS WHILE HUNTING FOR YOU, FURTHER TURNING THE POPULATION AGAINST THEM.

TARGET ENEMY SUPPLIES.

INVADERS GENERALLY NEED TO SHIP IN MONEY, WEAPONS, AND FOOD FROM FAR AWAY.

FIND OUT WHEN THEIR SHIPMENTS ARE ARRIVING, AND AMBUSH THEM!

YOU'RE SUPPLYING YOUR OWN MEN AND DEPRIVING THE ENEMY AT THE SAME TIME. BONUS!

AND LAST, BUT NOT LEAST, **NEVER GIVE UP!** THE CAUSE IS **NOT DEAD** SO LONG AS EVEN ONE **TRUE BELIEVER** YET LIVES!

SOME OF THE GREATEST REVOLUTIONS IN HISTORY LOOKED DOOMED FOR **YEARS**, BUT THEY CLUNG ON, LIVED TO FIGHT ANOTHER DAY, AND EVENTUALLY **SUCCEEDED!**

NOT YOURS THOUGH.

OK, SURE. THE POINT STILL STANDS...

NOW, LET'S MEET THE RELUCTANT REBEL WHO HOLDS THE RECORD FOR THE SHORTEST REIGN OF ANY ENGLISH SOVEREIGN.
IT'S THE MOMENTARY MONARCH, THE FLASH IN A SASH, THE TIME-TRIAL TUDOR, THE 9-DAY QUEEN...
JANE GREY!
JANE GREY
ENGLISH QUEEN
1537–1554

JANE, YOU MIGHT ALSO BE ENGLAND'S MOST RELUCTANT MONARCH— YOU HAD NO DESIRE WHATSOEVER TO BECOME QUEEN!
GOD NO!

WHEN THEY SPRUNG IT ON ME, I WAS SO FREAKED OUT I BURST INTO TEARS!

YOU MEAN YOU DIDN'T EVEN KNOW YOU WERE BEING MADE QUEEN?
TOTALLY BLINDSIDED ME!

I DIDN'T EVEN KNOW THE KING WAS DEAD! AND EVEN THEN, I'D HAVE ASSUMED ONE OF HIS SISTERS WOULD GET IT...

OK, WHOA, WHOA. BACK UP A MINUTE. WHAT KING IS THIS?

YEAH, I'M SORRY—IT'S A BIT COMPLICATED...

THE WHOLE MESS IS THANKS TO MY GRANDUNCLE **HENRY VIII**, SINCE HE DIVORCED HIS FIRST WIFE AND BEHEADED HIS SECOND.

WIFE NUMBER 3

THE KING **I** KNEW WAS HIS SON, **EDWARD VI**, BUT HE DIED YOUNG AND CHILDLESS.

AW WHAT!?
RELAX... WE'RE BOTH DEAD ALREADY...
EDWARD

HENRY ALSO HAD TWO **DAUGHTERS**, BUT KING EDWARD HAD SPECIFICALLY BANNED THEM FROM BECOMING QUEEN BECAUSE OF THE WHOLE DIVORCE/ BEHEADING THING.

HEY, NICE ONE, BRO!

ALSO MARY WAS A CATHOLIC, SO **EVERYONE** WANTED TO KEEP **HER** OFF THE THRONE. WHICH JUST LEFT **ME**...

GRR...
WATCH IT, YOU!

BUT NO ONE EXPECTED EDWARD TO DIE, SO NO ONE EXPECTED ME TO HAVE ANY CHANCE AT THE THRONE.

YUP, I WAS JUST PLAIN OL' LADY JANE FOR MOST OF MY LIFE.
BUT THAT WAS NEVER ENOUGH FOR YOUR PARENTS...

GOD, WHAT A NIGHTMARE! ALL THEY EVER THOUGHT ABOUT WAS GETTING ME MARRIED TO SOME RICH LORD!

NO MATTER WHAT I WAS DOING, IT WAS NEVER GOOD ENOUGH FOR THEM.

JANE! WRONG KNIFE!
JANE! SIT UP STRAIGHT!
JANE! DON'T BREATHE!
GOOD GRIEF! NO ONE WILL EVER WANT TO MARRY YOU!

GEEZ. SOUNDS PRETTY ROUGH.
YEAH—ALL I EVER REALLY WANTED WAS TO BE LEFT ALONE WITH MY READING.

IT WAS MY ONE REFUGE. BUT EVEN **THAT** DIDN'T LAST...
JANE!
GOOD NEWS...

WE'VE ARRANGED FOR YOU TO MARRY **LORD GUILFORD DUDLEY**!
HIS DAD IS THE RICHEST LORD IN ENGLAND!

I WAS SO **MISERABLE**! I DIDN'T **LOVE** DUDLEY. I DIDN'T EVEN **KNOW** HIM!

THEN ONE DAY I WAS SUMMONED TO COURT...
UH. HEY GUYS. WHAT'S GOING ON?
...OH.

I **BEGGED** THEM TO JUST LEAVE ME ALONE, BUT THEY INSISTED KING EDWARD HAD CHOSEN **ME** TO BE **QUEEN** BEFORE HE DIED, AND I HAD TO ACCEPT IT.

BUT THEN...
SO... UH... NOW YOU'RE QUEEN... I GET TO BE KING, RIGHT?
HUSBAND, DUDLEY JR.

SUDDENLY, IT HIT ME! IT WAS ALL A **SET-UP**!

REMEMBER **DUDLEY** SR. WAS THE RICHEST AND MOST POWERFUL LORD IN ENGLAND...

HE KNEW THE KING WAS DYING, SO HE'D ARRANGED MY MARRIAGE, **AND** GOT THE KING TO NOMINATE ME...
JANE? GOOD IDEA. AT LEAST SHE'S NOT A **CATHOLIC**.
THAT'S RIGHT, YOUR MAJESTY.

ALL SO HIS DUMMY OF A SON COULD BECOME **KING**!
NO **WAY**. YOU CAN BE A **DUKE** IF YOU LIKE.
WAAAH!
I'M TELLING MOMMY!

BUT HE REALLY HAD SOMETHING TO CRY ABOUT SOON ENOUGH! TURNS OUT THE PEOPLE DIDN'T **WANT** SOME GIRL THEY'D NEVER HEARD OF AS QUEEN...

THEY DIDN'T CARE ABOUT SOME ABSTRACT LEGITIMACY DISPUTE!
WHO **IS** THIS GREY GIRL?
MARY IS HENRY'S DAUGHTER. MAKE **HER** QUEEN!

MARY CAME MARCHING IN WITH A HUGE ARMY OF SUPPORTERS AND BOOM! MY 9-DAY REIGN WAS OVER.

YOU KNOW, YOU MIGHT HAVE ACHIEVED **LESS** THAN ANYONE I'VE EVER HAD ON THIS SHOW...

GIVE ME A BREAK! I'D LIKE TO SEE HOW **YOU'D** HAVE DONE, AGED **16**, AGAINST THE MOST POWERFUL PEOPLE IN THE COUNTRY!

IT WAS ACTUALLY PRETTY NICE.

I WASN'T IN A CELL OR ANYTHING... I HAD NICE ROOMS, I COULD READ IN THE GARDENS, AND I WASN'T BOTHERED BY MY HUSBAND OR HIS AWFUL FAMILY (THEY WERE TOO BUSY GETTING EXECUTED).

OOH HOO HOO HO...
CHOP!

IN FACT, IF IT WASN'T FOR ALL THE BEHEADING, IT WOULD'VE BEEN THE HAPPIEST TIME OF MY LIFE.
BUT IT WASN'T LONG BEFORE IT WAS YOUR TURN...

EVEN THOUGH I NEVER EVEN **WANTED** THE CROWN, QUEEN MARY DECIDED I WAS TOO MUCH OF A **THREAT**.

I'M SORRY M'LADY

I FORGIVE YOU, EXECUTIONER. JUST MAKE IT QUICK.

I TRIED REALLY HARD TO ACT COOL, BUT WHEN I COULDN'T FIND THE EXECUTION BLOCK, I STARTED TO PANIC.
AH! WHERE IS IT!?

I GUESS YOU MIGHT SAY THAT YOU LOST YOUR HEAD...?
YOU'VE MADE THAT JOKE BEFORE, HAVEN'T YOU?

THE WHITE TOWER
9-DAY QUEEN LADY JANE GREY WAS HELD PRISONER IN THE TOWER OF LONDON, SO I THOUGHT SHE'D BE THE PEREFCT GUIDE...
I ACTUALLY HAD QUITE A NICE STAY THERE. UNTIL, YOU KNOW...
THE ORIGINAL TOWER WAS BUILT BY WILLIAM THE CONQUEROR, SHORTLY AFTER 1066, TO DEFEND AGAINST THE RECENTLY CONQUERED PEOPLE OF LONDON.
YAH! TRY AND GET ME NOW, YOU ANGLO-SAXON PUNKS!
THE WHITE TOWER, THE CENTRAL DONJON INSIDE THE CASTLE, GOT ITS NAME AFTER IT WAS WAS WHITEWASHED BY HENRY III.
HENRY VII'S PERSONAL GUARDS WERE THE FIRST BEEFEATERS, (THE COLORFULLY DRESSED WARDERS OF THE TOWER).
AS PART OF THEIR SALARY, THEY COULD EAT AS MUCH BEEF AS THEY WANTED FROM THE KING'S TABLE, HENCE THE NAME.
YOU MISSED A SPOT.
PARDON ME, YER MAJ.
-HIC!- FOUND IT...
I'LL NEVER TAL-AAAGH!
MANY WENT INTO THE TOWER, BUT FEW CAME OUT. ALTHOUGH AT LEAST ONE JAILBREAK IS RECORDED: IN 1101, RANULF FLAMBARD, BISHOP OF DURHAM, ESCAPED OUT OF A WINDOW USING A ROPE THAT HIS FRIENDS HAD SMUGGLED IN TO HIM INSIDE A WINE BARREL.
ORIGINALLY A FORTRESS, THE TOWER ONLY LATER BECAME A PRISON—FAMOUS PRISONERS INCLUDE GUY FAWKES, WHO WAS TORTURED IN THE DREADED TOWER DUNGEON.

LEGEND HAS IT THAT SIX RAVENS MUST BE KEPT AT THE TOWER, OR ENGLAND WILL BE DESTROYED.
CHARLES II SUPPOSEDLY WANTED TO REMOVE THE RAVENS, AFTER HIS ROYAL ASTRONOMER COMPLAINED THEY WERE POOPING ON HIS TELESCOPES.
BUT WHEN HE WAS WARNED OF THE LEGEND, HE AGREED TO MOVE THE OBSERVATORY INSTEAD, FOUNDING THE ROYAL OBSERVATORY AT GREENWICH, ENGLAND.
EITHER THE BIRDS GO, OR I DO!
THE TOWER IS NOW MOST FAMOUS AS THE BUILDING WHERE THE CROWN JEWELS ARE KEPT—THEIR VALUE IS ESTIMATED TO BE MORE THAN $5 BILLION!
EDWARD I STARTED STORING THE ROYAL TREASURES IN THE TOWER IN 1303, AFTER THEY WERE STOLEN FROM THEIR PREVIOUS HOME IN WESTMINISTER ABBEY.
YOU GUYS HAD ONE JOB!
SEVERAL GHOSTS ARE SAID TO HAUNT THE TOWER, INCLUDING THOSE OF ANNE BOLEYN (BEHEADED BY HUSBAND, HENRY VIII), HENRY VI (CLUBBED WHILE PRAYING IN THE CHAPEL), THE PRINCES IN THE TOWER (IMPRISONED AND LIKELY STARVED BY THEIR UNCLE, RICHARD III), AND LADY JANE GREY (THAT'S ME!).
WOOOO!
THERE'S EVEN THE GHOST OF A GRIZZLY BEAR, WHICH WAS PART OF THE TOWER MENAGERIE AND IS SUPPOSED TO HAVE SCARED SEVERAL TOURISTS TO DEATH!
I MEAN, COME ON! HOW IS ONE SUPPOSED TO COMPETE WITH THAT!?

MY GUEST THIS WEEK IS A REBEL IN MORE WAYS THAN ONE— A WARRIOR WOMAN WHO LIVED BY HER OWN RULES, ALL THE WHILE FIGHTING THE SLOW DESTRUCTION OF TRADITIONAL IRISH CULTURE.
PLEASE WELCOME THE SWASHBUCKLING SOVEREIGN OF THE FIGHTING IRISH, THE PIRATE QUEEN OF CONNAUGHT...
GRÁINNE NÍ MHÁILLE!*
GRAINNE NI MHAILLE
PIRATE QUEEN
1530 – c.1603

GRAINNE, AS THE DAUGHTER OF A MINOR IRISH SEA-CHIEFTAIN, YOU GOT YOUR SEA-LEGS EARLY.
WELL, MY DAD COMMANDED A SMALL TRADING FLEET...

I WANTED TO GO SAILING TOO, BUT DAD WAS ALWAYS SENDING ME OFF WITH SOME EXCUSE...
NO WAY! YOUR, ER... HAIR... MIGHT GET CAUGHT IN THE RIGGING.
YEAH...

AND SO, THE NEXT DAY...

*ROUGHLY: GRAW-NYEH NEE WAW-YEH. (IN ENGLISH, GRACE O'MALLEY)

AFTER THAT **CLOSE SHAVE**, HE HAD TO TAKE ME!
YOUR COURAGE AND SKILL SOON MADE YOU A FAVORITE WITH THE SAILORS.

AND MY HABIT OF SAVING THEIR LIVES! ONE TIME WE WERE UNDER ATTACK FROM PIRATES, AND GETTING THE WORST OF IT...

UNTIL I PULLED OFF A CRUSHING DEATH-FROM-ABOVE **ELBOW SMASH** OFF THE TOP RIGGING, TURNING THE BATTLE.

BUT YOUR **HAIR-RAISING** ADVENTURES ALMOST CAME TO AN END WHEN YOU WERE MARRIED OFF TO THE SON OF ANOTHER LOCAL CLAN: DONAL "SON OF BATTLE" O'FLAHERTY.

THAT'S JUST HOW IT WORKED BACK THEN. THE O'FLAHERTYS HAD MORE LAND, MORE SHIPS, MORE CASTLES, SO IT WAS A STEP UP FOR OUR LITTLE CLAN.

BUT DONAL "SON OF BATTLE" LIVED UP TO HIS NAME—HE WAS ALWAYS OFF PICKING FIGHTS. SO **I** ENDED UP RUNNING THE O'FLAHERTY CLAN LANDS, SHIPS, **AND** CASTLES.

IN THE END HE PICKED A FIGHT WITH THE WRONG NEIGHBORS AND GOT HIMSELF KILLED.

I AVENGED HIM, OF COURSE, BUT HIS CLAN COULDN'T HANDLE A WOMAN RUNNING THE SHOW, SO THEY KICKED ME OUT! AFTER **19** YEARS OF DEDICATED SERVICE TOO...

SO WITH NOTHING BUT A FEW LOYAL FOLLOWERS, AND SOME ROCK-SOLID ADMIN EXPERIENCE, YOU RETURNED TO YOUR OLD CASTLE, BECOMING QUEEN OF A TINY STRIP OF ATLANTIC COAST.

YEAH, NOT FOR LONG THOUGH... I IMMEDIATELY GOT TO WORK BUILDING THAT TINY KINGDOM INTO A MIGHTY PIRATE EMPIRE.

FIRST I SUPPLEMENTED MY MEAGER FORCES WITH **GALLOWGLASS** MERCENARIES FROM SCOTLAND, BASICALLY A TERRIFYING CROSS BETWEEN HIGHLANDERS AND VIKINGS.

BACKED BY THESE HIGHLAND HARD-MEN, I STARTED COLLECTING TOLLS FROM WHOEVER WANTED TO SAIL THROUGH OUR WATERS.

AND IF THEY DIDN'T WANT TO PAY, WELL, OK. WE'D JUST TAKE IT THE HARD WAY...

AS YOUR EMPIRE EXPANDED, YOUR NEWLY WON PIRATE QUEEN STATUS COMMANDED AN APPROPRIATE DEGREE OF **RESPECT**.
AND I EXPECTED TO GET IT!

ONE TIME I STOPPED BY A LOCAL EARL'S CASTLE FOR SOME DINNER, BUT HE REFUSED TO LET ME IN!
ER, SORRY. WE'RE, UM, NOT HERE...?

THAT'S A TERRIBLE INSULT TO A PROUD IRISH QUEEN!
SO I KIDNAPPED HIS SON UNTIL HE APOLOGIZED AND AGREED TO FEED ME **WHENEVER** I WANTED.

LITERALLY, HE HAD TO HAVE AN **EXTRA PLACE** SET FOR ME AT ALL MEALS, IN CASE I HAPPENED TO DROP BY.
JUST CHECKING...

YOU ALSO FOUND TIME TO GET MARRIED TO ANOTHER LOCAL LORD, THOUGH HE DIDN'T LAST TOO LONG.
WELL, IRISH LAW LET COUPLES TEST-DRIVE A MARRIAGE FOR A YEAR—THEY CALLED IT THE "ONE YEAR CERTAIN" SYSTEM.

BUT AFTER A YEAR, I WAS **CERTAIN** I DIDN'T WANT HIM. SO I JUST CHANGED ALL THE LOCKS ON HIS CASTLE, CHUCKED HIS STUFF IN THE MOAT, AND DUMPED HIM FROM THE BATTLEMENTS!

HE DID GIVE ME A SON, THOUGH, WHO WAS BORN AT SEA DURING A PARTICULARLY FEROCIOUS ATTACK BY RIVAL PIRATES.

MY GUYS WERE LOSING SO I HAD TO RUN OUT AND FIGHT THEM OFF MYSELF.
DO I HAVE TO DO **EVERYTHING** AROUND HERE?!

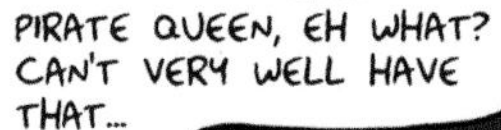
EVENTUALLY, YOUR PIRATICAL ANTICS BECAME TOO MUCH FOR THE ENGLISH GOVERNOR.

PIRATE QUEEN, EH WHAT? CAN'T VERY WELL HAVE THAT...

HEY LOOK, PIRATING YOUR NEIGHBORS WAS BASICALLY AN UNAVOIDABLE WAY OF LIFE BACK THEN. HIS **REAL** ISSUE WAS BECAUSE I REFUSED TO SUBMIT TO ENGLISH RULE!

AT THIS TIME, THE ENGLISH QUEEN **ELIZABETH I** WAS TRYING TO FORCE ALL THE IRISH CHIEFTAINS TO ACCEPT HER AS THEIR OVERLORD.

THOSE WHO AGREED HAD TO GIVE UP THEIR TRADITIONAL CUSTOMS: LANGUAGE, LAWS, CLOTHES, AND EVEN RELIGION.

THOSE WHO RESISTED GOT, WELL, WHAT I GOT. MY LANDS WERE BURNED, MY SHIPS CONFISCATED, AND MY PORTS CLOSED.

I FOUGHT BACK WITH EVERYTHING I HAD, BUT THEN THEY WENT FOR MY FAMILY. MY ELDEST SON GOT TRICKED AND EXECUTED, MY MIDDLE SON BETRAYED **ME** AND SIDED WITH THE ENGLISH...

OOH, I WAS SO MAD! I INVADED HIS LANDS, THE UNGRATEFUL WRETCH, BURNED HIS FIELDS, AND REFUSED TO SPEAK TO HIM EVER AGAIN.

WHICH MADE **CHRISTMAS** AWKWARD...

TELL MY **SO-CALLED** SON TO PASS THE GRAVY. OR I'LL SET HIS SPROUTS ALIGHT.

BUT WHEN MY YOUNGEST SON WAS IMPRISONED, I HAD ONLY ONE OPTION LEFT. I SAILED TO LONDON TO PUT MY CASE TO ELIZABETH, QUEEN TO QUEEN.

OK, IT DIDN'T GET OFF TO A GREAT START, AFTER THEY FOUND MY **HIDDEN DAGGER**, BUT I EXPLAINED THAT'S JUST WHAT **ALL** PIRATE QUEENS CARRY IN THEIR UNDERWEAR.

ALSO I REFUSED TO BOW TO HER, SINCE WE WERE BOTH QUEENS. **AND** SHE HAD TO DO THE WHOLE MEETING IN LATIN SINCE THERE WAS NO WAY I WAS GOING TO SPEAK **ENGLISH**.

THINKING ABOUT IT, IT'S A MIRACLE SHE DIDN'T HAVE ME **EXECUTED**...

BUT INSTEAD SHE AGREED TO RELEASE MY SON AND FIRE THAT IDIOT GOVERNOR.

AND I WAS ABLE TO CARRY ON PIRATING, SO LONG AS I ONLY PIRATED HER ENEMIES.

WOW. YOU MUST'VE REALLY DRIVEN AN **ARR'D** BARGAIN!

RIGHT?

BECAUSE PIRATES SAY...

OK, OK! I GET IT!

A FEAST FIT FOR A QUEEN
PARTY-HEARTY PIRATE QUEEN GRÁINNE NÍ MHÁILLE HAS INVITED US ALL TO A BANQUET!
AND WHAT BETTER WAY TO TAKE A PEEK INTO THE LOST WORLD OF TUDOR-ERA IRELAND.
LEADING THE FEAST, OF COURSE, WAS THE CLAN CHIEFTAIN.
THAT'S ME!
CLAN CHIEFS WERE ELECTED FROM THE EXTENDED FAMILY OF THE PREVIOUS CHIEF.
WHICH SOUNDS SURPRISINGLY DEMOCRATIC, UNTIL YOU REALIZE THE JOB ALMOST ALWAYS WENT TO THE GUY WITH THE BIGGEST ARMY.
MOST OF THE POPULATION WERE EITHER FARMERS, NOMADIC CATTLE HERDERS, OR LANDLESS PEASANTS.
YEAH, THOSE GUYS DIDN'T USUALLY GET INVITED TO FANCY PARTIES. BUT THEY DID PROVIDE THE FOOD.
BEEF WAS THE MAIN SOURCE OF MEAT, BUT IT WAS ONLY EATEN ON SPECIAL OCCASIONS—MOSTLY, CATTLE WERE KEPT FOR MILK AND CHEESE.
MEAT WAS ROASTED OR BOILED AND SERVED GLAZED WITH HONEY AND SALT.
FOR A MOVABLE FEAST LIKE THIS ONE, MEAT MIGHT BE BOILED IN A TEMPORARY CAULDRON MADE FROM THE COW'S OWN HIDE.
UNDER THE TRADITIONAL IRISH LAW, A COOK WAS NOT RESPONSIBLE FOR PEOPLE GETTING SCALDED BY HOT STEWS, AS LONG AS HE SHOUTED A LOUD ENOUGH WARNING.

THE CHIEF WAS SURROUNDED BY THEIR FINE, AN EXTENDED FAMILY GROUP ALL CLAIMING DESCENT FROM THE SAME LEGENDARY ANCESTOR.
MY CLAN CLAIMED DESCENT FROM SOME DUDE NAMED MAILLE SO WE WERE THE PEOPLE OF MAILLE, OR O'MALLEY IN ENGLISH.
A BIT LIKE KNIGHTS, THE FINE WERE SUPPOSED TO FIGHT FOR THE CHIEF, COLLECT HIS RENTS, AND GENERALLY KEEP EVERYONE IN LINE.
THE IRISH LORDS MOSTLY LIVED IN DISTINCTIVE FORTIFIED TOWER HOUSES.
BUT IN THE SUMMER, WE PREFERRED TO EAT OUTSIDE, ALFRESCO STYLE!
DINNER WAS SERVED ON LONG, LOW TABLES, WITH THE GUESTS SITTING ON CUSHIONS OR STRAW.
THE TOP FORM OF ENTERTAINMENT WERE THE BARDS. THEIR JOB WAS RECITING EPIC POEMS ABOUT THEIR LORD'S GREAT DEEDS, AND THE HEROES OF THE PAST.
ALTHOUGH, THEY ALSO MADE UP INSULTING POEMS ABOUT THE LORD'S ENEMIES AND HOW BADLY THEY SUCKED.
MUSICIANS, LIKE HARPISTS AND BAGPIPERS, WERE ALSO POPULAR.
AS WERE, ER, PROFESSIONAL FARTERS.
NOTHING LIKE A GOOD OL' BUTT BURP CONCERT TO REALLY COMPLETE A DINNER PARTY...
HOLD ON, FARTING WAS ACTUALLY A JOB?
MAN, I KNEW I WAS BORN IN THE WRONG TIME PERIOD!

OUR NEXT INCENDIARY INSURGENT IS BRITAIN'S FAVORITE PARLIAMENTARY PYROMANIAC!
PLEASE GIVE AN EXPLOSIVE WELCOME TO THE MAN WITH THE DYNAMITE PLAN...
GUY FAWKES!
GUY FAWKES
CONSPIRATOR
1570–1606

GUY, YOUR TOTAL FAILURE TO BLOW UP PARLIAMENT ON NOVEMBER 5TH, 1605 IS STILL CELEBRATED EACH YEAR WITH BONFIRES AND FIREWORKS.

HOW DOES IT FEEL TO BE COMMEMORATED AS HISTORY'S MOST PATHETIC, UNMITIGATED BUNGLER?
VERILY, THAT'S A BIT HARSH!

OK, IT DIDN'T WORK OUT, BUT IT WAS A GOOD PLAN! WE JUST HAD A STROKE OF BAD LUCK...

THERE'S NO SUCH THING AS BAD LUCK, ONLY **POOR PREPARATIONS**. AND I PUT IT TO YOU THAT YOUR "PLOT" WAS THE MOST POORLY PREPARED, SHODDY, FLOP OF A PLAN IMAGINABLE!

THEN, WHEN THE KING ARRIVES, IT'S BOOM-TIME!
BOO!

THEN, WHILE I'M ESCAPING TO FRANCE, YOU OTHERS START A REBELLION!
HA HA

WE KIDNAP THE KING'S DAUGHTER, THE PRINCESS, AND CROWN HER THE NEW QUEEN.
BOO!

THEN, WE GET HER TO MARRY A CATHOLIC LORD, AND ALL OUR PROBLEMS ARE SOLVED! ANY QUESTIONS?
NONE!
WHAT CAN POSSIBLY GO WRONG!?

PLENTY! LIKE WHAT IF SHE DIDN'T WANT TO MARRY A CATHOLIC LORD? ESPECIALLY SINCE YOU GUYS JUST BLEW UP HER DAD!

IT COULD'VE WORKED...
IT DIDN'T WORK! YOU DIDN'T EVEN GET TO THAT PART OF YOUR CRACKPOT PLAN, BECAUSE YOU KEPT MESSING IT UP!

FIRST YOU GAVE UP ON THE TUNNEL...
MAN, THIS IS HARD WORK!
THERE HAS TO BE AN EASIER WAY...

TURNS OUT, THERE WERE ABANDONED CELLARS UNDER THE PARLIAMENT. WE JUST HAD TO RENT ONE OUT. MUCH EASIER!
FIREWOOD
GUNPOWDER
THERE! PERFECT!

IN FACT, MAYBE A LITTLE TOO EASY, HUH?
AHEM! WELL, SURE, EASY TO SAY THAT NOW...

THEN THE WHOLE THING HAD TO BE POSTPONED...
THEY DELAYED PARLIAMENT BECAUSE OF THE PLAGUE! YOU THINK I SHOULD'VE PLANNED FOR THAT!?

A TRUE PROFESSIONAL PREPARES FOR EVERYTHING...

AND YOU ALL STARTED GETTING COLD FEET...
WELL, WHAT IF WE BLEW UP SOME OF OUR FRIENDS? THERE WERE SOME CATHOLIC LORDS WHO WERE GOING TO BE THERE...

SO YOU WROTE TO THEM...
My lord,
I can't say what, but something bad is going to happen. You might want to avoid Parliament for a while...
p.s. please don't show this to the King... (Boo!)

SO OBVIOUSLY, THEY SHOWED IT TO THE KING!
BOO!

HIS GUARDS SEARCHED PARLIAMENT, INCLUDING THE CELLARS, AND WHO DID THEY FIND, SKULKING AROUND WITH A POCKETWATCH, A BOX OF MATCHES, AND A LONG FUSE...

YOUR WHOLE GANG WAS CAPTURED, TORTURED, AND PUT TO DEATH. THE GUNPOWDER PLOT WAS OVER...

AND EVEN WHILE YOU WERE STILL ALIVE, ALL OVER THE COUNTRY PEOPLE WERE LIGHTING BONFIRES TO CELEBRATE.
OH LOOK! FIREWORKS!

AND THE TRADITION CONTINUES TO THIS DAY, REMINDING US ALL OF THE DANGERS OF POOR PLANNING AND THE IMPORTANCE OF BEING PREPARED!
FSSSH!
FSSH!
FSSH!

FSSSH

SHOULD'VE BEEN PREPARED FOR THAT...

GUNPOWDER, TREASON, AND PLOT

FAILED FIREBRAND GUY FAWKES PLANNED TO PAINT THE TOWN RED ON THE ORIGINAL BONFIRE NIGHT!
AND WHILE IT DIDN'T QUITE WORK OUT, HIS EXPLOSIVE PLAN VERY NEARLY WENT OFF WITH A BANG!

-SIGH- AND WE WERE SO CLOSE...
THE EVIL KING JAMES I (BOO!) WAS PERSECUTING CATHOLICS THROUGHOUT BRITAIN...
SOMETHING HAD TO BE DONE!

OUR PLAN WAS TO BLOW HIM UP, ALONG WITH ALL HIS MINISTERS, AT THE HOUSE OF LORDS.
KING'S ENTRANCE
HI, CHAPS, WHAT'S UP?
KING
NOTHING EXPLODE-Y I HOPE?
THRONE
BISHOPS HAVE THEIR OWN SPECIAL ENTRANCE HERE

CELLAR
GUNPOWDER
WE STASHED 36 BARRELS OF THE STUFF DIRECTLY UNDER THE KING'S THRONE—ENOUGH TO REDUCE THE ENTIRE BUILDING TO RUBBLE!

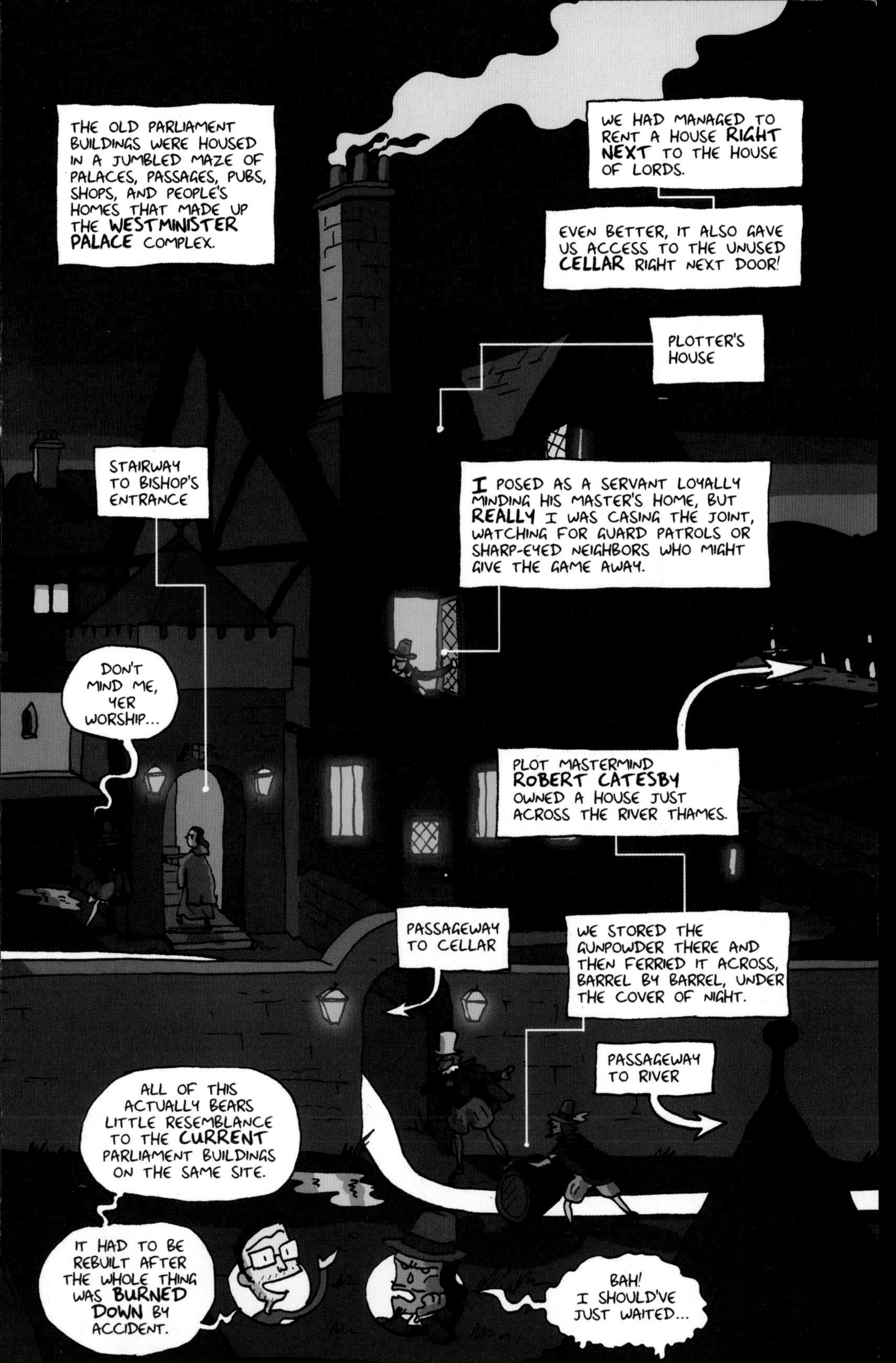
THE OLD PARLIAMENT BUILDINGS WERE HOUSED IN A JUMBLED MAZE OF PALACES, PASSAGES, PUBS, SHOPS, AND PEOPLE'S HOMES THAT MADE UP THE WESTMINISTER PALACE COMPLEX.
WE HAD MANAGED TO RENT A HOUSE RIGHT NEXT TO THE HOUSE OF LORDS.
EVEN BETTER, IT ALSO GAVE US ACCESS TO THE UNUSED CELLAR RIGHT NEXT DOOR!
PLOTTER'S HOUSE
STAIRWAY TO BISHOP'S ENTRANCE
I POSED AS A SERVANT LOYALLY MINDING HIS MASTER'S HOME, BUT REALLY I WAS CASING THE JOINT, WATCHING FOR GUARD PATROLS OR SHARP-EYED NEIGHBORS WHO MIGHT GIVE THE GAME AWAY.
DON'T MIND ME, YER WORSHIP...
PLOT MASTERMIND ROBERT CATESBY OWNED A HOUSE JUST ACROSS THE RIVER THAMES.
PASSAGEWAY TO CELLAR
WE STORED THE GUNPOWDER THERE AND THEN FERRIED IT ACROSS, BARREL BY BARREL, UNDER THE COVER OF NIGHT.
PASSAGEWAY TO RIVER
ALL OF THIS ACTUALLY BEARS LITTLE RESEMBLANCE TO THE CURRENT PARLIAMENT BUILDINGS ON THE SAME SITE.
IT HAD TO BE REBUILT AFTER THE WHOLE THING WAS BURNED DOWN BY ACCIDENT.
BAH! I SHOULD'VE JUST WAITED...

NOW FOR ONE OF THE MOST **CONTROVERSIAL** REBELS IN ENGLISH HISTORY! WAS HE AN INSANE DICTATOR, DRUNK WITH POWER, OR THE FOUNDER OF MODERN DEMOCRACY? OR **BOTH**!
GET READY FOR A **WARTS-AND-ALL** LOOK AT...
OLIVER CROMWELL!
OLIVER CROMWELL
MILITARY DICTATOR
1599–1658

CROMWELL, YOU ARE REMEMBERED AS THE MOST IMPORTANT FIGURE OF THE **ENGLISH CIVIL WAR**. WHAT WAS ALL THE FIGHTING ABOUT?

THE FIGHTING WAS BECAUSE KING CHARLES I WAS A TOTAL **POOP-HEAD**!
CORPSE TALK: ALWAYS A BALANCED VIEW...

OH, COME ON! HE WAS ALWAYS ABUSING HIS POWER, MAKING UP NEW LAWS AND TAXES JUST SO HE COULD GET RICH.

WELL, I'M THE KING! I CAN DO WHAT I LIKE! AFTER ALL, I WAS APPOINTED BY GOD.

NO, YOU WERE APPOINTED TO SERVE GOD'S PEOPLE. YOU HAVE TO GET PARLIAMENT'S PERMISSION FOR ALL THESE TAXES...
OH PIFFLE!

I'LL GET MY ARMY, AND WE'LL SHOW YOU!
OH YEAH! WELL, MY ARMY'S WAY BETTER THAN YOURS!

THE KING'S SUPPORTERS, ALSO CALLED THE CAVALIERS, WERE LAZY AND POORLY DISCIPLINED.

A BATTLE? OK, HOLD ON. I'LL BE RIGHT THERE...

BUT MY GUYS (CALLED ROUNDHEADS BECAUSE OF THEIR SHORT HAIRSTYLES) WERE DISCIPLINED, HIGHLY TRAINED, AND PUMPED UP ON THE WORD OF GOD!
WOO!

I RECRUITED THEM EXCLUSIVELY FROM AMONG THE PURITANS—HARDCORE CHRISTIANS WHO BELIEVED IN A RIGID, MORALLY PURE CHURCH. LIKE ME!

SINCE WE KNEW GOD WAS ON OUR SIDE, WE WENT INTO BATTLE FEARLESSLY AND JOYOUSLY.
WHO ARE THESE GUYS!?
ON-WARD CHRISTIAN SO-O-LDIERS...

WAIT. GOD WAS ON YOUR SIDE? HOW DID YOU... UM... KNOW?

I WON! IF GOD WASN'T ON MY SIDE, I'D HAVE LOST.

AH! CAN'T ARGUE WITH THAT, CAN YOU?
I... UH...
HM.

WE CAPTURED THE KING AND MADE HIM PROMISE TO BEHAVE.
I'M VERY SORRY. I WON'T DO IT AGAIN...

BUT HE WAS LYING! RIGHT AWAY HE ESCAPED AND WENT BACK TO WAR AGAIN.
HAD MY FINGERS CROSSED!

MAN, SERIOUSLY! HOW DO YOU REASON WITH A GUY LIKE THAT!?
SO YOU DECIDED TO KILL HIM.

IT WASN'T JUST MY DECISION! HE WAS TRIED AND FOUND GUILTY OF TREASON!

RIGHT, BUT YOUR ARMY KEPT HIS SUPPORTERS AWAY FROM THE TRIAL.

YES, OK, THAT HELPED. BUT HE HAD TO DIE. THE WAR WOULD NEVER HAVE ENDED OTHERWISE.

THEN YOU WENT AFTER HIS SON, WHO WAS HIDING OUT IN IRELAND.
NOT HIDING! STARTING ANOTHER WAR!

WELL, YOU SURE PUT A STOP TO THAT! YOU KILLED SO MANY PEOPLE THAT THE IRISH STILL USE YOUR NAME AS A SWEAR WORD!

THEY... WHAT? REALLY!?
YEAH. LIKE "WHAT A TOTAL CROMWELL" OR "OH, CROMWELL"!

HA! THAT'S PRETTY COOL.
THE IRISH DON'T THINK IT'S COOL! THOSE GUYS HATE YOU!
MEH. CAN'T PLEASE EVERYONE.

WELL, YOU DIDN'T PLEASE ANYONE!
THAT'S NOT TRUE. I KEPT THE PURITANS PRETTY HAPPY...

AND THE ONE THING THAT MADE PURITANS REALLY HAPPY WAS STOPPING EVERYONE ELSE'S FUN!

YOU GOT RID OF ALL THE OLD **FEAST** DAYS AND INTRODUCED **FAST** DAYS INSTEAD.

OH BOY!

SWEARING WAS ILLEGAL...

OH, CROMWELL!
OOP!

AS WAS MAKEUP. YOU HAD ROAMING SQUADS OF SOLDIERS TO SCRUB THE FACES OF WOMEN CAUGHT WEARING IT!

YOU BANNED DRINKING, COCK-FIGHTING, BEAR-BAITING, GAMBLING, AND GOING TO THE THEATER...

YOU EVEN BANNED **CHRISTMAS**. COME ON. THAT'S JUST **MEAN**!

LOOK. HAVING FUN WAS AN EVIL DISTRACTION, KEEPING PEOPLE FROM WHAT THEY SHOULD'VE BEEN DOING.

WHICH WAS...?

READING THE **BIBLE**.

NEEDLESS TO SAY, YOU BECAME ENORMOUSLY UNPOPULAR.
CAN'T THINK WHY...

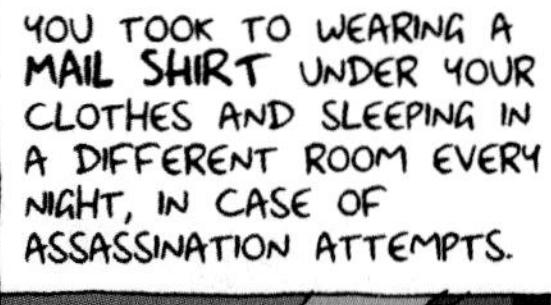

YOU TOOK TO WEARING A MAIL SHIRT UNDER YOUR CLOTHES AND SLEEPING IN A DIFFERENT ROOM EVERY NIGHT, IN CASE OF ASSASSINATION ATTEMPTS.

BUT YOU FOILED THEM BY DYING FIRST!
HEH! PRETTY TRICKY, HUH?

ROUNDHEADS VS CAVALIERS

MY NEW MODEL ARMY WAS DESIGNED TO BE THE OPPOSITE OF ALL OF THAT!
THEY CALLED US THE ROUNDHEADS.
ON ACCOUNT OF OUR SHORT HAIR.
BUT YOU'VE GOT LONG HAIR.
I'M OLIVER CROMWELL— I DID WHAT I LIKED.
BUT THERE'S THIS PART IN THE BIBLE WHERE IT SAYS MEN SHOULD CUT THEIR HAIR SHORT. SO THAT'S WHAT THEY ALL STARTED DOING...
WHAT CAN I SAY? WE WERE REALLY INTO THE BIBLE...
ANYWAY, IN MY ARMY, SOLDIERS WERE PROMOTED BECAUSE THEY WERE GOOD AT THE JOB, NOT BECAUSE OF WHO THEIR DADDY WAS.
SO OUR GENERALS WERE BETTER.
PARLIAMENT BOUGHT EQUIPMENT IN BULK, SO ALL SOLDIERS GOT THE WEAPONS THEY NEEDED.
THEY ALSO ALL WORE THE SAME RED COATS SO AT LAST WE COULD AVOID SHOOTING OUR OWN GUYS.
BUT OF COURSE, THE BIGGEST THING WAS MORALE.
MY GUYS BELIEVED THEY WERE FIGHTING TO BUILD A NEW KINGDOM OF GOD ON EARTH.
IT GAVE THEM THE COURAGE TO RUN UPHILL INTO A HAIL OF BULLETS. SINGING HYMNS WHILE THEY DID IT.
LIKE I SAID. WE WERE REALLY INTO THE BIBLE...

MY NEXT GUEST MIGHT JUST BE THE MOST MORALLY MINDED MASS MURDERER IN THE WHOLE OF HISTORY, AN INDEFATIGABLE IDEALIST WHO WENT FROM RIGHTEOUS REVOLUTIONARY TO TYRANNOSAURUS OF TERROR IN A MATTER OF MONTHS...
PLEASE WELCOME THE FRENCH REVOLUTION'S DAPPER DECAPITATOR...
MAXIMILIEN ROBESPIERRE!
MAXIMILIEN ROBESPIERRE
REVOLUTIONARY
1758–1794

ROBESPIERRE, YOU CAME TO POWER IN THE FRENCH REVOLUTION: THE REVOLUTION THAT REWROTE THE REVOLUTIONARY RULEBOOK; OVERTHROWING THE OLD ORDER AND PLUNGING FRANCE INTO A NIGHTMARE OF BLOOD AND TERROR.

SO WHAT GOT YOU STARTED ON THE REVOLUTIONARY ROAD?
WELL, REALLY, I JUST WANTED TO HELP PEOPLE.

AND THE POOR PEOPLE OF PRE-REVOLUTIONARY FRANCE NEEDED ALL THE HELP THEY COULD GET!

UNFAIR AND HARD-TO-UNDERSTAND LAWS MADE IT POSSIBLE FOR RICH NOBLES TO BULLY, EXPLOIT, AND STEAL FROM THE POOR.

I BECAME A LAWYER TO BRING JUSTICE TO THOSE TOO POOR AND DOWNTRODDEN TO GET HELP ANYWHERE ELSE.

I COULDV'E BEEN A JUDGE (A MUCH BETTER-PAYING JOB) BUT I COULDN'T FACE HAVING TO SENTENCE PEOPLE TO DEATH.
A BARBARIC PRACTICE— UNFIT FOR AN ENLIGHTENED NATION LIKE FRANCE.

AND SO, THERE I MIGHT HAVE STAYED, SELFLESSLY TOILING AWAY AS A POOR COUNTRY LAWYER.
IF IT HADN'T BEEN FOR THE KING...
THE KING?

LOUIS XVI. HE WAS ALSO HAVING TROUBLE WITH THE NOBLES, SINCE ONE OF THEIR MAIN PRIVILEGES WAS THAT THEY COULD COLLECT ALL THESE TAXES BUT THEY DIDN'T HAVE TO PAY ANY TO HIM!

AFTER YEARS OF BAD DECISIONS AND TERRIBLE HARVESTS, THE KING HAD NO MONEY TO RUN THE COUNTRY, AND THE POOR DIDN'T EVEN HAVE MONEY TO BUY FOOD. IT WAS A FULL-ON NATIONAL DISASTER.

THE KING TRIED TO PASS NEW LAWS, REQUIRING THE NOBLES TO PAY TAXES TOO, BUT HE NEEDED PARLIAMENT'S APPROVAL. A PARLIAMENT MADE UP OF ALL THESE SAME NOBLES.
SORRY, YOUR MAJ, BUT THAT'S A HARD NON, MERCI...

SO HE DECIDED TO TRY CALLING AN ANCIENT FORM OF THE PARLIAMENT, ONE THAT HADN'T BEEN USED FOR CENTURIES, THAT INCLUDED NOBLES, THE CHURCHMEN, AND THE COMMON PEOPLE.

I MANAGED TO GET MYSELF ELECTED AS A REPRESENTATIVE OF THE COMMON PEOPLE. THIS WAS MY CHANCE, NOT JUST TO FIGHT UNFAIR LAWS, BUT TO CHANGE THEM.

THE KING'S PLAN WAS TO GET US COMMONERS TO VOTE THROUGH HIS NEW LAWS, DESPITE THE NOBLES' OBJECTIONS.
BRILLIANT! IT CAN'T FAIL...

BUT WHEN WE ALL GOT TOGETHER, WE STARTED TO THINK THAT, YOU KNOW WHAT? US COMMONERS WERE BETTER PLACED TO DECIDE WHAT FRANCE NEEDED THAN THE NOBLES OR THE KING.
YEAH!
HEAR HEAR!

WE DECLARED OURSELVES THE LEGITIMATE GOVERNMENT, WHICH DIDN'T GO DOWN TOO WELL WITH LOUIS.
THEY DID WHAT!?

HE SENT IN THE **ARMY** TO TRY AND INTIMIDATE US BACK INTO LINE.
THOSE UNGRATEFUL PEASANTS! I'LL SHOW 'EM...

WHICH DROVE THE POOR PEOPLE OF PARIS **NUTS**! JUST WHEN THEY'D GOTTEN A PARLIAMENT THAT MIGHT ACTUALLY CARE ABOUT **THEM**, IT WAS GOING TO BE DESTROYED.

IT WAS ACTUALLY AN OLD SCHOOL-FRIEND OF MINE, **CAMILLE DESMOULINS**, WHO SPARKED THE PARIS REBELLION.
ARE WE GONNA PUT UP WITH THIS!? I'D RATHER **DIE**!

AN ANGRY MOB FORMED, RANSACKING EVERY BLACKSMITH'S AND WEAPONS SHOP IN THE CITY, EVEN PLUNDERING GUNPOWDER FROM THE **BASTILLE**, THE ANCIENT FORTRESS OF PARIS.

WITH A HEAVILY ARMED REVOLUTIONARY MOB NOW IN CONTROL OF THE CAPITAL, THE KING DECIDED A GOVERNMENT OF COMMONERS WAS A GREAT IDEA AFTER ALL.

NOW IN CONTROL OF THE COUNTRY, THE NEW PARLIAMENT LOST NO TIME ABOLISHING UNJUST LAWS, STRIPPING AWAY UNFAIR ARISTOCRATIC PRIVILEGES, AND USHERING IN A NEW ERA OF **FREEDOM**, **EQUALITY**, AND **BROTHERHOOD**.

BUT THE GOOD VIBES DIDN'T LAST LONG...
WELL, THERE WAS STILL THE WHOLE PROBLEM OF WHAT TO DO WITH THE KING...

I MEAN, WE **TRIED** TO WORK WITH HIM, AND HE **CLAIMED** HE WAS COMMITTED TO IDEALS OF THE REVOLUTION...

BUT THEN WE CAUGHT HIM TRYING TO SNEAK OFF TO VISIT HIS IN-LAWS, THE **AUSTRIANS**.
THAT SOUNDS... ALL RIGHT..? NICE FAMILY VISIT...

THE **REASON** HE WAS SNEAKING OFF WAS TO BRING IN AN AUSTRIAN **ARMY** TO **SLAUGHTER** HIS OWN PEOPLE AND MAKE HIMSELF AN ABSOLUTE MONARCH AGAIN!

I ARGUED THAT AS LONG AS THE KING WAS ALIVE HE COULD NEVER BE TRUSTED. THERE WOULD ALWAYS BE PLOTS TO PUT HIM BACK ON THE THRONE.

AND SO, TO ENSURE THE SAFETY OF THE REVOLUTION, LOUIS XVI WAS SENT TO THAT NEWLY INVENTED ENGINE OF ENLIGHTENED EXECUTION, THE GUILLOTINE.

UM, WHAT HAPPENED TO YOUR WHOLE "THE DEATH PENALTY IS BARBARIC" THING?
THAT WAS FOR REGULAR CRIMES! A TOTALLY DIFFERENT THING!
TOTALLY.

THE REVOLUTION WAS AN UNPRECEDENTED ATTEMPT TO BUILD AN ABSOLUTELY FAIR AND JUST SOCIETY. ANY THREATS TO ITS SUCCESS HAD TO BE REMOVED—FOR THE GOOD OF EVERYONE!

AND WE WERE SURROUNDED BY THREATS. EXILED NOBLES HAD TEAMED UP WITH BASICALLY ALL OF FRANCE'S NEIGHBORS AND WERE INVADING FROM EVERY DIRECTION, WHILE MASSIVE REVOLTS PLUNGED THE COUNTRYSIDE INTO CHAOS.

BUT BY RECRUITING EVERY ABLE-BODIED YOUNG MAN IN FRANCE, WE WERE ABLE TO RAISE AN ABSOLUTELY HUGE ARMY AND BEAT THEM ALL!
DO IT FOR THE REVOLUTION!
OR GET GUILLOTINED. YOUR CHOICE...

...JUST ONE OF THE MANY INCREDIBLE INNOVATIONS OF THE NEWLY FORMED COMMITTEE OF PUBLIC SAFETY OF WHICH, AHEM, I WAS A LEADING MEMBER...

COMMITTEE OF PUBLIC SAFETY? SOUNDS KINDA BORING.
AU CONTRAIRE! IT WAS OUR JOB TO DO WHATEVER IT TOOK TO KEEP THE PRECIOUS REVOLUTION SAFE.

BUT WHAT I REALLY WANTED TO STAMP OUT WERE INSIDIOUS INTERNAL THREATS: PEOPLE WHO PRETENDED TO BE ON BOARD WITH THE REVOLUTION WHILE WORKING SECRETLY TO DESTROY IT...

FOREIGN SPIES, SECRET FANS OF THE KING TRYING TO BRING BACK THE MONARCHY, RICH PEOPLE TRYING TO HOLD ON TO THEIR ILL-GOTTEN WEALTH...

POOR PEOPLE PUSHING TO GET TOO MUCH OF THE RICH PEOPLE'S WEALTH, CORRUPT CHEATS LOOKING TO SELL OUT THE REVOLUTION TO MAKE A QUICK BUCK...

ONLY WHEN **EVERY LAST ONE** OF THEM HAD BEEN SENT TO THE GUILLOTINE COULD FRANCE FINALLY BECOME A GLORIOUS **REPUBLIC OF VIRTUE**.

AND SO, IN YOUR RELENTLESS QUEST FOR **VIRTUE**, YOU BEGAN THE INFAMOUS **REIGN OF TERROR**.
TERROR IS JUST SWIFT, INFLEXIBLE JUSTICE...

NOT EVEN **DESMOULINS**, YOUR OLD FRIEND, AND INSTIGATOR OF THE STORMING OF THE BASTILLE, WAS SPARED YOUR BRAND OF JUSTICE.

HEY, I **TRIED** TO GET HIM LET OFF! BUT, WELL, HE SHOULDN'T HAVE CRITICIZED THE COMMITTEE!
ANY DISUNITY OR DISSENT WAS A THREAT TO THE REVOLUTION.

AT THE HEIGHT OF THE TERROR, THE COMMITTEE WAS CHOPPING OFF MORE THAN **50** HEADS **PER DAY**.

WE'RE GONNA NEED A BIGGER BASKET...

BUT THAT WAS KIND OF THE PROBLEM. THERE WERE SO **MANY** PLOTS THAT IT WAS TAKING **FOREVER**! ALL THE TRIALS, EVIDENCE, WITNESSES— WE DIDN'T HAVE **TIME** FOR THAT!

SO WE PASSED A LAW DITCHING ALL THAT JUNK. IF A COMMITTEE MEMBER THOUGHT SOMEONE WAS HATCHING A PLOT... BOOM!
GOOD ENOUGH.

BUT WITH THE NEW, NONEXISTENT STANDARD OF EVIDENCE, PEOPLE COULD JUST **MAKE STUFF UP**.

MAD AT YOUR NEIGHBOR? JEALOUS OF THAT WOMAN WITH INCREDIBLE HAIR? JUST CLAIM THEY'VE BEEN COMPLAINING ABOUT THE NEW GOVERNMENT AND IT'S OFF TO THE CHOP.

HEH HEH.
CHOP.
CHOP.
CHOP.

WHAT? LOOK, I **TRIED** TO REIN IT IN!
A BIT...

WE HAD THESE ROAMING DELEGATES WHO WENT OUT TO THE PROVINCES TO BRING TERROR TO ANY ENEMIES OF THE REVOLUTION OUT THERE...

AND SOME OF THEM WERE PRETTY BRUTAL. I RECALLED THEM ALL AND STARTED AN INQUIRY INTO THE WORST OF THEIR EXCESSES.

WHICH DIDN'T GO DOWN TOO WELL WITH THEM. ONE GUY TRIED TO UNDERMINE ME BY SPREADING A RUMOR I WAS GOING TO MAKE MYSELF A DIVINELY ORDAINED DICTATOR!

AND? WERE YOU?

SHEER NONSENSE. I MEAN... OKAY, I HAD THE POWER OF LIFE AND DEATH OVER MILLIONS.

AND, OKAY, IN MY CAPACITY AS MORAL GUARDIAN OF THE NATION I HAD JUST INVENTED A NEW RELIGION.
YOU WHAT NOW?

THE CULT OF THE SUPREME BEING! UNDER MY INSPIRED LEADERSHIP, IT WOULD SWEEP OUT THE OLD OPPRESSIVE SUPERSTITIONS, AND USHER IN A NEW LOVE OF VIRTUE, REASON, AND THE DIVINE ARCHITECT OF THE UNIVERSE.

OH, AND, OKAY, IT'S ALSO TRUE I WAS PLANNING A MASSIVE PURGE TO GET RID OF ANY OF MY ENEMIES STILL REMAINING IN THE PARLIAMENT.

BUT I THINK I SHOWED ADMIRABLE RESTRAINT. I WARNED THEM ALL IT WAS COMING, BUT WITHOUT NAMING ANY NAMES.

WELL, THAT "RESTRAINT" MIGHT HAVE BEEN YOUR UNDOING, SINCE EVERY GUY IN THERE FIGURED HE COULD BE ON THAT ENEMIES LIST.

ABANDONED BY EVEN THE FEW FRIENDS YOU HAD LEFT, YOU WERE DENOUNCED, ARRESTED, AND CONDEMNED.

IN THE END, YOU ENDED YOUR LIFE AS JUST ONE MORE VICTIM OF THE TERRIBLE MACHINE TO WHICH YOU HAD CONDEMNED SO MANY.

I GUESS IN THE END ALL THAT POWER WENT TO YOUR...
WHAT? WENT TO MY WHAT?

THE FRENCH REVOLUTIONARY LEADERS, LIKE MAXIMILIEN ROBESPIERRE, WANTED TO IMPROVE ALL ASPECTS OF SOCIETY.
LIKE THEY INVENTED NEW RATIONAL WEIGHTS AND MEASURES LIKE THE METER AND THE KILOGRAM, WHICH WE STILL USE.
AND A NEW, RATIONAL CALENDAR, COMPLETE WITH RATIONAL, 10-DAY WEEKS, WHICH WE DON'T.
YEEAH... PEOPLE WERE NOT THRILLED TO ONLY GET A WEEKEND EVERY 10 DAYS.
SINCE WE'D DITCHED THE OLD CHRISTIAN FESTIVALS, LIKE CHRISTMAS AND EASTER, WE NEEDED SOME NEW ONES. SO I ORGANIZED A MASSIVE CEREMONY...
THE FESTIVAL OF THE SUPREME BEING!
THE WHOLE THING BEGAN AT THE TUILERIES PALACE (WHERE THE LOUVRE MUSEUM IS NOW), WHERE WE BURNED A GIANT STATUE OF ATHEISM TO REVEAL ANOTHER STATUE OF WISDOM HIDDEN INSIDE.
THEN ONLOOKERS CHEERED AND THREW CONFETTI AS A MASSIVE PROCESSION OF CITIZENS WOUND ITS WAY THROUGH PARIS TO THE CHAMPS DE MARS (WHERE THE EIFFEL TOWER NOW STANDS).
THERE THEY FOUND THE CENTERPIECE OF THE NEW CEREMONY, AN ENORMOUS, PAPER-MACHE MOUNTAIN.

BUT THEIR MOST CONTROVERSIAL INNOVATION WAS IN RELIGION.
SOME OF THE EARLY REVOLUTIONARIES WANTED TO DITCH IT ENTIRELY, CREATING THE ATHEIST CULT OF REASON.
BUT I ARGUED THAT PEOPLE NEED GOD TO GIVE THEM HOPE AND INSPIRE THEM TO BECOME BETTER PEOPLE.
SO (AFTER I'D HAD ALL THE ATHEISTS GUILLOTINED), I INVENTED A NEW RELIGION, COMBINING LOVE OF GOD WITH CIVIC VIRTUES, LIKE OBEDIENCE, HARD WORK, AND LOVE OF COUNTRY.
A GIANT STATUE OF HERCULES (SYMBOL OF THE REVOLUTION) HOLDING ALOFT A SMALLER STATUE OF LIBERTY (SYMBOL OF -ER- LIBERTY...)
MEMBERS OF PARLIAMENT CLIMBED THE MOUNTAIN TO SING THE NEW FRENCH NATIONAL ANTHEM, LA MARSEILLAISE.
AND THEN, IN THE ABSOLUTE HIGHLIGHT OF THE CEREMONY, I DESCENDED FROM THE MOUNTAIN LIKE A NEW MOSES, TO DELIVER THE NEW REVOLUTIONARY COMMANDMENTS OF LIBERTE, EGALITE, FRATERNITE.
BREVITE. YOUR CULT LASTED HOW LONG?
6 WEEKS.
GEEZ. CAN'T A GUY HAVE HIS DAY IN THE SUN...?

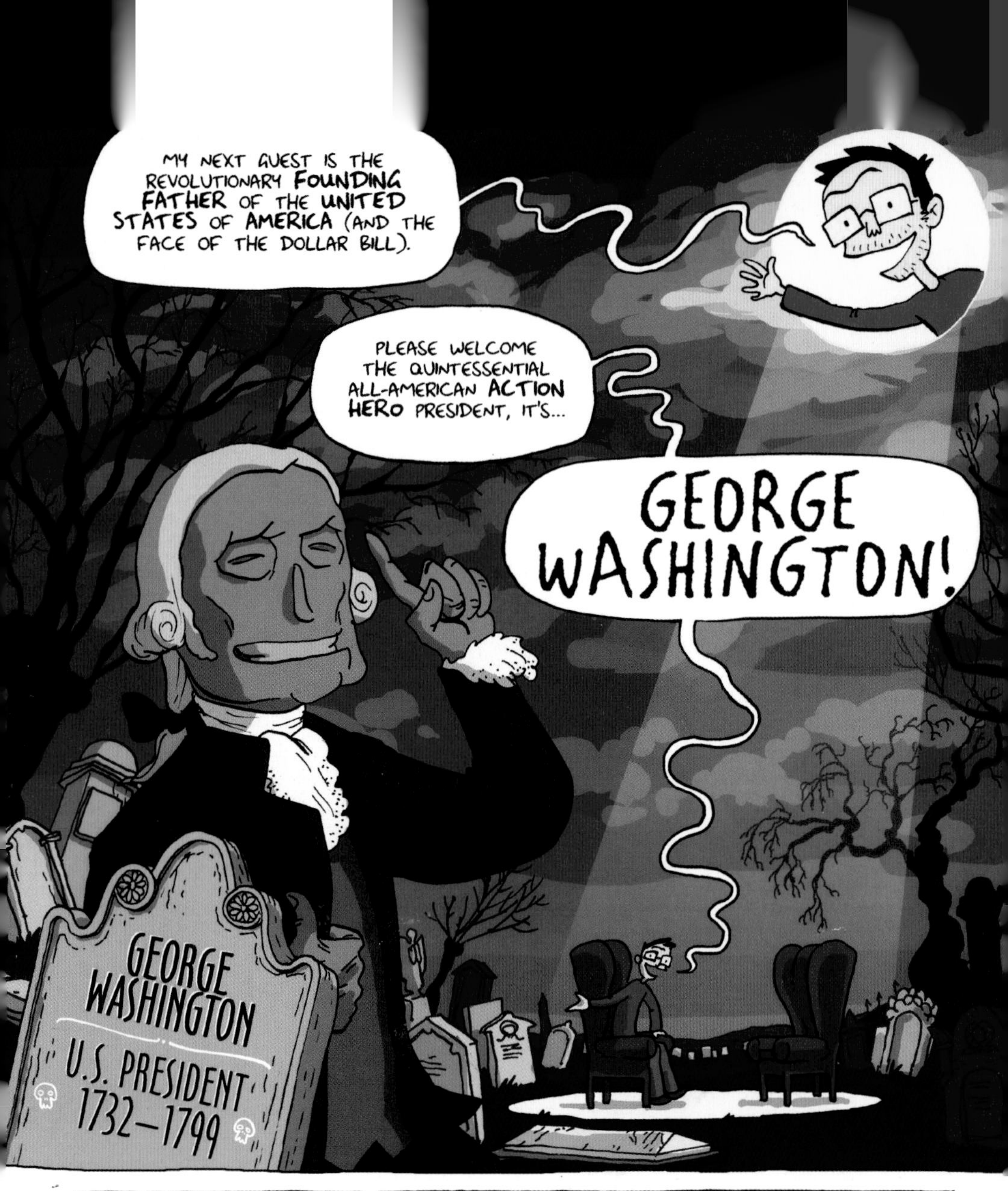
MY NEXT GUEST IS THE REVOLUTIONARY **FOUNDING FATHER** OF THE **UNITED STATES** OF **AMERICA** (AND THE FACE OF THE DOLLAR BILL).
PLEASE WELCOME THE QUINTESSENTIAL ALL-AMERICAN **ACTION HERO** PRESIDENT, IT'S...
GEORGE WASHINGTON!
GEORGE WASHINGTON
U.S. PRESIDENT
1732–1799

WASHINGTON, TO THIS DAY, YOU'RE PROBABLY AMERICA'S BEST KNOWN AND BEST LOVED PRESIDENT. AMERICAN SCHOOLKIDS LEARN BY HEART THE STORIES OF YOUR COURAGE, STRENGTH, AND HONESTY, LIKE THE STORY OF THE CHERRY TREE.

WHAT CHERRY TREE?

YOU CUT DOWN YOUR FATHER'S CHERRY TREE, JUST FOR KICKS, I GUESS, BUT WHEN HE CONFRONTED YOU, YOU WERE **SO HONEST** YOU ADMITTED IT...

I CANNOT TELL A LIE...

YEEAH...
NEVER HAPPENED.

AW MAN! REALLY?
I CANNOT TELL A LIE.
WELL, WHAT ABOUT YOUR LEGENDARY FEATS OF STRENGTH!?

LIKE, HOW YOU ONCE THREW A SILVER DOLLAR ACROSS THE POTOMAC RIVER!

THAT'S PRETTY INCREDIBLE.
TOTALLY INCREDIBLE, SINCE THE SILVER DOLLAR HADN'T BEEN INVENTED YET...

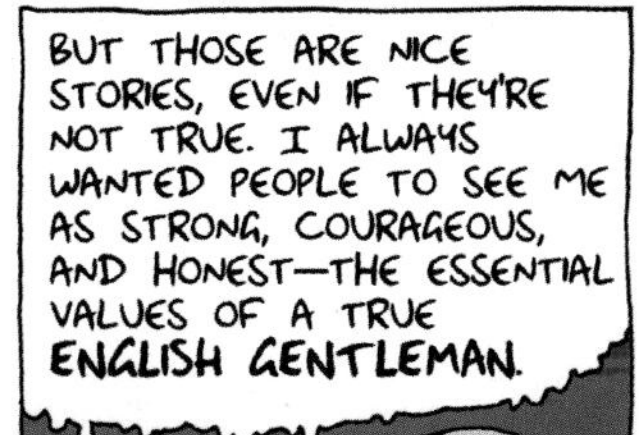
BUT THOSE ARE NICE STORIES, EVEN IF THEY'RE NOT TRUE. I ALWAYS WANTED PEOPLE TO SEE ME AS STRONG, COURAGEOUS, AND HONEST—THE ESSENTIAL VALUES OF A TRUE **ENGLISH GENTLEMAN**.

BUT... AREN'T YOU **AMERICAN**!?
AMERICA HADN'T BEEN INVENTED YET. WE WERE JOLLY WELL ENGLISH, WHAT, WHAT!
RA-THER.
TOODLE-PIP...

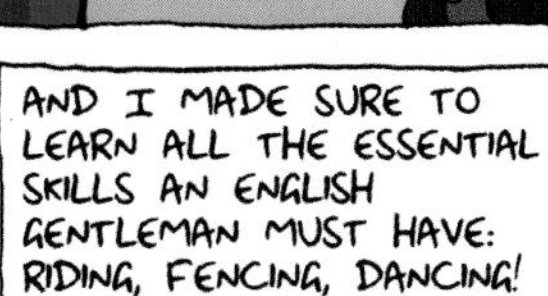
AND I MADE SURE TO LEARN ALL THE ESSENTIAL SKILLS AN ENGLISH GENTLEMAN MUST HAVE: RIDING, FENCING, DANCING!

AND OF COURSE, MY **FAVORITE** GENTLEMANLY PASTIME: **FIGHTING**! LIKE A TRUE ENGLISHMAN, I SIGNED UP TO FIGHT THE **FRENCH** DURING THE SEVEN YEARS WAR...

LIKE ALL GENTLEMEN OFFICERS, I DRESSED THE PART WITH A TOTALLY SWEET UNIFORM. (I DESIGNED IT MYSELF!).

BUT EVEN YOUR AWESOME FASHION SENSE WASN'T ENOUGH TO ATTAIN THE **ULTIMATE** SYMBOL OF GENTLEMANSHIP, A ROYAL COMMISSION IN THE **BRITISH ARMY**.

FRIGHTFULLY SORRY, OLD BEAN. **REAL** ENGLISHMEN ONLY...
HAW HAW!

SO YOU FIGURED IF YOU CAN'T JOIN 'EM, **BEAT 'EM**!

WELL, IT TURNS OUT, **LOTS** OF THE COLONISTS THOUGHT THE ENGLISH WERE JERKS.

THOSE ENGLISH ARE **JERKS**!

LIKE, **TOTALLY**.

THE ENGLISH HAD STARTED IMPOSING ALL SORTS OF UNFAIR **TAXES**...

IT'S NOT FAIR!
BUT WHAT ARE WE GOING TO **DO** ABOUT IT?!

WHOA! LOOK AT **THAT** GUY!

THAT IS ONE **SWEET** UNIFORM!

WE SHOULD PUT **HIM** IN CHARGE...

HEY! IT WASN'T **JUST** MY AMAZING OUTFITS THAT GOT ME ELECTED COMMANDER-IN-CHIEF OF THE REVOLUTIONARY ARMY! I WAS ALSO A **SUPERB** MILITARY STRATEGIST...

REALLY? BECAUSE I HEARD YOU LOST BATTLES **TWICE** AS OFTEN AS YOU WON. THAT'S NOT A GREAT TRACK RECORD...

OH COME ON!

OUR ENEMIES WERE A WELL-FED, WELL-DRESSED, WELL-EQUIPPED, PROFESSIONAL ARMY, FIGHTING FOR THE MOST POWERFUL MAN IN THE WORLD... THE KING OF ENGLAND!

MY GUYS WERE A BEDRAGGLED GROUP OF VOLUNTEERS WITH NO GUNPOWDER, NO SHOES, NO MONEY, AND NO MILITARY EXPERIENCE.

BUT I REALIZED WE DIDN'T **HAVE** TO WIN ALL THE BATTLES. WE JUST HAD TO **NOT GIVE UP**!

I HELD MY MEN TOGETHER THROUGH DEFEAT AND DREADFUL CONDITIONS BY REMINDING THEM WHAT WE WERE FIGHTING FOR: LIBERTY AND JUSTICE FOR ALL!

AND I USED INNOVATIVE TACTICS, LIKE CROSSING THE DELAWARE RIVER AT NIGHT, IN A BLIZZARD, TO CATCH OUR ENEMIES UNAWARES.

THEY'LL NEVER SEE US COMING!

MY MEN GREW TOUGHER, AND MORE DISCIPLINED. MORALE INCREASED...

SUPPLIES STARTED ROLLING IN FROM ENGLAND'S GREAT ENEMIES, THE FRENCH.
'ERE. 'AVE SOME MUSKETS...
AH 'OPE ZEY KEEL MANY EENGLISH, NON?

AND IN THE END, THE ENGLISH GAVE UP AND WENT HOME!
JOLLY WELL NOT WORTH IT, WHAT?
BALLY YANKEE DOODLES...

YOU WERE THE HERO OF THE NEWLY BORN NATION: THE UNITED STATES OF AMERICA!

YOU BECAME SO POPULAR, PEOPLE STARTED SUGGESTING YOU SHOULD BE KING.

I TOLD THEM NOT TO BE SILLY—WE'D JUST GOTTEN RID OF A KING, WE DIDN'T NEED ANOTHER ONE...

BUT WE NEEDED SOMEONE IN CHARGE. OTHERWISE NOTHING WOULD EVER GET DONE.

SO WE INVENTED THE OFFICE OF PRESIDENT.

A LEADER WHO WAS NOT DETERMINED BY BIRTHRIGHT, BUT SOMEONE WHO WOULD BE ELECTED BY THE PEOPLE.

AND THEY WANTED TO ELECT SOMEONE HONORABLE, SOMEONE TRUSTWORTHY, SOMEONE WELL-DRESSED, SOMEONE TALL...

AND YOU FIT THE BILL!
GEDDIT? BILL? LIKE DOLLAR BILL...
I GET IT...

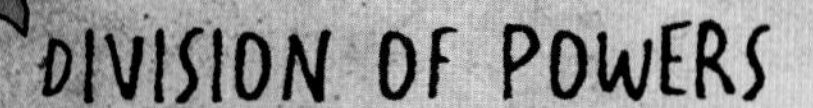
DIVISION OF POWERS

AFTER WINNING THE REVOLUTIONARY WAR OF INDEPENDENCE, GO-GETTER GENERAL GEORGE WASHINGTON FAMOUSLY TRIED TO RETIRE.
BUT INSTEAD I GOT HAULED OUT TO OVERSEE THE WRITING OF THE NEW COUNTRY'S FOUNDATIONAL DOCUMENT, THE U.S. CONSTITUTION.

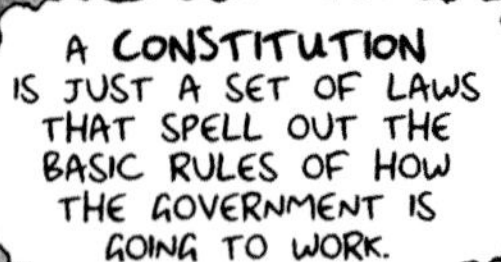
A CONSTITUTION IS JUST A SET OF LAWS THAT SPELL OUT THE BASIC RULES OF HOW THE GOVERNMENT IS GOING TO WORK.

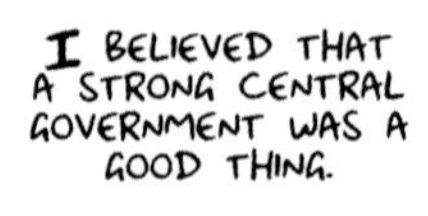
I BELIEVED THAT A STRONG CENTRAL GOVERNMENT WAS A GOOD THING.
THE PRESIDENT WAS NOT A KING SINCE WE'D JUST FINISHED FIGHTING A WAR SPECIFICALLY TO GET RID OF THE KING.

SO WE DEVELOPED A SYSTEM OF CHECKS AND BALANCES, WHERE EACH BRANCH OF THE GOVERNMENT IS IN CHARGE OF DIFFERENT THINGS, AND MAKES SURE THE OTHER PARTS PLAY NICE.

THE LEGISLATIVE BRANCH IS THE TWO HOUSES OF CONGRESS.

THE SENATE...
AND THE HOUSE OF REPRESENTATIVES.

THEY COME UP WITH NEW LAWS, AND IF BOTH HOUSES AGREE ON THEM, THEY TAKE THEM TO THE PRESIDENT FOR SIGNING.

THEY ALSO HAVE THE POWER TO IMPEACH THE PRESIDENT AND EVEN KICK HIM OUT OF OFFICE IF HE GETS OUT OF LINE.

CONGRESS CAN ALSO PUT FORWARD AMENDMENTS TO THE CONSTITUTION—REVISIONS THAT ADD NEW PARTS OR CHANGE WHAT'S IN THERE ALREADY.

FOR EXAMPLE, THE 13TH AMENDMENT FINALLY ABOLISHED SLAVERY IN 1865.
OH GOOD, I HOPED THEY'D DO AWAY WITH THAT—NASTY BUSINESS.

YOU OWNED 317 SLAVES!
I SET THEM ALL FREE!
AFTER I WAS DEAD, SURE, BUT STILL...

THE **EXECUTIVE BRANCH** IS BASICALLY THE **PRESIDENT**.

I NOBLY AND DUTIFULLY AGREED TO BE ELECTED THE FIRST ONE...

THE PRESIDENT IS THE **ELECTED** LEADER, BUT ONLY FOR **4** YEARS, AFTER WHICH THERE'S ANOTHER ELECTION.

THE PRESIDENT IS IN CHARGE OF MAKING **PEACE OR WAR** WITH OTHER COUNTRIES.

AND THEIR **SIGNATURE** IS REQUIRED TO MAKE LAWS OFFICIAL, WHICH MEANS THEY CAN ALSO **VETO** (BLOCK) LAWS THEY DON'T LIKE.

I BELIEVED THE PRESIDENT ALSO HAS A RESPONSIBILITY AS A SORT OF NATIONAL **ROLE MODEL**, SO I TRIED TO DEMONSTRATE THE SORT OF DIGNIFIED, HONORABLE BEHAVIOR I WANTED TO SEE IN OTHERS.

THE **JUDICIAL BRANCH** IS THE **COURTS**.

THEY ARE THE **JUDGES** WHO INTERPRET WHAT THE LAW MEANS IN ACTUAL TRIALS.

AT THE VERY TOP IS THE **SUPREME COURT**, WHICH JUDGES THOSE CASES TOO DIFFICULT OR IMPORTANT FOR THE OTHERS TO HANDLE.

THEY ARE APPOINTED BY THE PRESIDENT, BUT HAVE TO BE APPROVED BY THE SENATE.

THEY CAN ALSO **BLOCK** THE PRESIDENT OR CONGRESS FROM DOING SOMETHING **UNCONSTITUTIONAL** (BREAKING THE RULES IN THE CONSTITUTION).

LOTS OF COUNTRIES IN THE WORLD HAVE A CONSTITUTION...

BUT THE U.S. CONSTITUTION WAS THE **FIRST** COMPLETELY WRITTEN NATIONAL CONSTITUTION, AND IT REMAINS THE OLDEST ONE **STILL IN USE**, ANYWHERE IN THE WORLD.

I GUESS IT WAS WORTH GETTING OUT OF YOUR BATHROBE AFTER ALL...

AND NOW LET'S MEET THE BUTT-KICKING BOOKWORM WHO FOUGHT THE FRENCH, SMASHED THE SPANISH, AND BASHED THE BRITISH TO FOUND THE WORLD'S FIRST (AND ONLY) FREE REPUBLIC OF FORMER SLAVES.
HE'S THE HEROIC HEAD HONCHO OF THE HAITIAN REVOLUTION, IT'S...
TOUSSAINT LOUVERTURE!
TOUSSAINT LOUVERTURE
REBEL LEADER
1743–1803

TOUSSAINT, YOU WERE BORN INTO PERHAPS THE MOST CRUEL, BRUTAL, AND INHUMAN OF ALL THE SLAVE COLONIES, FRENCH OCCUPIED SAINT-DOMINGUE. (LATER RESTORED TO ITS ORIGINAL NAME: HAITI.)

MORE THAN A MILLION AFRICANS WERE STOLEN FROM THEIR HOMES TO BE BEATEN, STARVED, OR WORKED TO DEATH ON HAITI'S HUGE SUGAR PLANTATIONS.

MOST DIED WITHIN 2 YEARS OF THEIR ARRIVAL, SINCE IT WAS CHEAPER TO JUST IMPORT NEW SLAVES THAN TO KEEP OLD ONES ALIVE.

I WAS ACTUALLY PRETTY LUCKY, IF YOU CAN EVER CALL A SLAVE "LUCKY." MY FATHER HAD BEEN A PRINCE BEFORE HE WAS CAPTURED AND SOLD BY HIS ENEMIES.

SO, WHILE I WAS STILL A SLAVE, I LEARNED TO READ AND WRITE, AND WAS GIVEN SOME OF THE BETTER JOBS. YOU KNOW, THE KIND THAT DIDN'T INVOLVE BEING WHIPPED ALL THE TIME...

PLUS YOU HAD ACCESS TO AN EXPENSIVE LIBRARY, WHICH ALLOWED YOU TO CONTINUE YOUR EDUCATION WITH SOME OF HISTORY'S GREATEST TEACHERS...

GUYS LIKE JULIUS CAESAR (MILITARY TACTICS), MACHIAVELLI (POLITICAL THEORY), AND EPICTETUS (THE GREEK STOIC PHILOSOPHER WHO HAD HIMSELF BEEN A SLAVE).

AND YOU ALSO DISCOVERED THE MORE RECENT THINKERS OF THE FRENCH ENLIGHTENMENT. GUYS LIKE ROUSSEAU, WHO ARGUED THAT ALL MEN ARE CREATED EQUAL.
WHICH BASICALLY PROVES THAT SLAVERY IS WRONG.
HMM. I WAS JUST THINKING THAT...

THAT MIGHT SEEM PRETTY OBVIOUS TO YOU NOW, BUT AT THE TIME IT WAS CONSIDERED A DANGEROUS IDEA.

DANGEROUS? HOW COULD EQUALITY BE DANGEROUS?
WELL, IT GOT THE FRENCH TO OVERTHROW THEIR ARISTOCRACY AND KILL THEIR KING. SO I GUESS IT WAS PRETTY DANGEROUS FOR THEM...

THE FRENCH REVOLUTION ALSO THREW HAITI INTO CHAOS, WITH PRO-REVOLUTION FOLKS FIGHTING SUPPORTERS OF THE MONARCHY.
VIVE LA FRANCE!
VIVE LE ROI!

AND THEN, TAKING ADVANTAGE OF THE CONFUSION, AN ESCAPED VODOU PRIEST NAMED DUTTY BOUKMAN COORDINATED A MASSIVE SLAVE REVOLT.

AT THE SAME EXACT MOMENT, SLAVES ACROSS HAITI ROSE UP, SET FIRE TO THE PLANTATIONS, GRABBED WHATEVER FARM TOOLS THEY COULD, AND TOOK THEIR VIOLENT REVENGE ON EVERY WHITE PERSON THEY COULD FIND.

FOR THREE WEEKS, THE SMOKE FROM BURNING PLANTATIONS BLOTTED OUT THE SUN.

THEY WAITED FOR ORDERS BEFORE ATTACKING, WHICH MEANT WE COULD PLAN AMBUSHES. AND AN ARMY DOESN'T KILL ENEMIES WHO SURRENDER, SO THEY WERE LESS LIKELY TO FIGHT TO THE DEATH.

THE SLAVE OWNERS STOPPED FIGHTING AND GANGED UP TO SUPPRESS THE REBELLION. BOUKMAN, THE REBEL LEADER, WAS CAPTURED AND HIS HEAD PUT ON A SPIKE.
SO DON'T GET ANY IDEAS...

THINGS WERE LOOKING BAD FOR THE REBELLION. THEY NEEDED A **LEADER**— SOMEONE WHO UNDERSTOOD THE TACTICS, POLITICS, AND PHILOSOPHY OF THE EUROPEANS.

UH. HELLO...?
I KNOW, RIGHT?

I STARTED SMALL, RECRUITING JUST A FEW HUNDRED MEN AND TRAINING THEM IN MILITARY TACTICS.

INSTEAD OF AN ANGRY MOB, THEY WERE BECOMING AN **ARMY**.

OVERWHELMED BY OUR NEWLY FORMED REBEL ARMY, OUR ENEMIES BEGAN TO SURRENDER.

AND I ALSO USED MY UNDERSTANDING OF POLITICS TO MAKE AN ALLIANCE WITH THE NEIGHBORING **SPANISH** (WHO HATED THE FRENCH) TO GET MY HANDS ON FRESH WEAPON SUPPLIES.

I WON BATTLE AFTER BATTLE, DEFEATING THE FRENCH **AND** MY ENEMIES AMONG THE REBELS, TO BECOME LEADER OF THE WHOLE EX-SLAVE ARMY.

BUT THEN, JUST WHEN YOU HAD THE FRENCH ALMOST COMPLETELY BEATEN, YOU SUDDENLY SWITCHED SIDES AND STARTED FIGHTING **FOR** THEM!
WHAT THE HECK, MAN?

WELL, IT WASN'T QUITE THE SAME FRENCH; A NEW, RADICAL GROUP HAD TAKEN OVER, AND THEY PROMISED TO ABOLISH SLAVERY COMPLETELY.

WHEREAS THE SPANISH REALLY JUST WANTED US TO BEAT THE FRENCH, SO THEY COULD COME IN, TAKE OVER, AND MAKE US ALL SLAVES AGAIN.

SO YOU FOUGHT OFF THE SPANISH...
AND THE BRITISH, WHO JUST SHOWED UP HOPING TO GRAB SOME LAND FOR THEMSELVES IN THE CONFUSION.

BUT THE OUTSIDE WORLD WAS EVEN MORE CONFUSING. IN THE CHAOS FOLLOWING THE FRENCH REVOLUTION, A RUTHLESS GENERAL NAMED NAPOLEON HAD TAKEN CONTROL.

HE WANTED TO RECONQUER THE ISLAND AND REINSTATE SLAVERY. NO WAY I WAS GOING TO LET THAT HAPPEN!

NAPOLEON'S ARMY WAS TOO BIG TO FIGHT HEAD-ON, SO ONCE AGAIN I GOT TACTICAL, HIDING IN THE MOUNTAINS, AND ALLOWING HORRIBLE TROPICAL DISEASES LIKE YELLOW FEVER TO TAKE THEM OUT FOR ME...

OOH. CUNNING...

BUT I WAS GETTING TIRED. I'D BEEN FIGHTING FOR 10 YEARS, BUT ALL I REALLY WANTED TO DO WAS RETIRE, HANG OUT WITH MY FAMILY, AND PUTTER IN MY GARDEN.

THE FRENCH OFFERED TO NEGOTIATE PEACE, BUT THEN HAD ME CAPTURED AND SHIPPED OFF TO DIE IN PRISON.

BUT I KNEW, EVEN IF THEY KILLED ME, THEY'D ONLY BE CUTTING DOWN THE TRUNK OF THE TREE OF FREEDOM! ITS ROOTS WERE TOO DEEP TO EVER BE DESTROYED...

THE HAITIAN PEOPLE CONTINUED THE FIGHT AND, WITHIN MONTHS OF YOUR DEATH, WON THEIR FREEDOM.
I GUESS YOU COULD SAY THEY JUST... WOODEN QUIT...?
TREE...? WOODEN...?
-SIGH-

EQUILATERAL ENSLAVEMENT

I SPOKE WITH **TOUISSAINT LOUVERTURE** ABOUT HIS STRUGGLE TO FREE THE SLAVES OF WHAT IS NOW **HAITI**. BUT WHAT WERE ALL THOSE SLAVES EVEN **DOING THERE** IN THE FIRST PLACE!?

RIGHT, WELL IN HAITI IT WAS MOSTLY ABOUT **SUGAR**. SOME MERCHANTS REALIZED THEY COULD MAKE A **FORTUNE** SELLING THE STUFF TO THE SWEET-TOOTHED EUROPEANS, AND SO THEY DEVELOPED SOMETHING CALLED THE **TRIANGULAR TRADE**.

MOST SLAVES ENDURED BACKBREAKING LABOR, CLEARING, PLANTING, TENDING, AND HARVESTING THE SUGARCANE FIELDS OF THE PLANTATIONS. MOST DIED WITHIN **10** YEARS FROM OVERWORK, DISEASE, AND CRUEL PUNISHMENTS FOR THE SMALLEST INFRACTIONS.

IN THE FINAL SIDE OF THE TRIANGLE, THE "**RETURN PASSAGE**," PLANTATION-PRODUCED SUGAR, COTTON, AND TOBACCO WERE SHIPPED BACK TO EUROPE TO BE PROCESSED AND SOLD, AND THE WHOLE CYCLE BEGAN AGAIN.

STOP 3: THE NEW WORLD

OVER **10 MILLION** AFRICANS WERE SHIPPED TO THE NEW WORLD AS SLAVES.

HALF A MILLION WENT TO NORTH AMERICA.

2 MILLION WENT TO BRITISH COLONIES LIKE JAMAICA.

1.5 MILLION WERE SHIPPED TO FRENCH SAINT-DOMINGUE (HAITI), INCLUDING MY PARENTS.

2.5 MILLION WENT TO THE MASSIVE SPANISH EMPIRE.

4 MILLION WENT TO THE PORTUGUESE EMPIRE, IN WHAT IS NOW BRAZIL.

THE MAGNIFICENT MAROONS

DESPITE THE HORRIBLE PUNISHMENTS IF THEY WERE CAUGHT, SOME SLAVES DID MANAGE TO ESCAPE INTO THE UNINHABITED MOUNTAINS OF JAMAICA AND HAITI, AND THE JUNGLES OF BRAZIL.

THE LARGEST OF THESE COMMUNITIES OF "MAROONS" (ESCAPED SLAVES) WAS THE **QUILOMBO DOS PALMARES** IN BRAZIL. AT ITS HEIGHT IT CONTAINED MORE THAN **20,000** PEOPLE WITH THEIR OWN KING.

BUT **MY** REBELLION WAS THE **ONLY ONE** THAT LED TO A PERMANENT, FREE COUNTRY OF FORMER SLAVES.

SLAVE TRADE

STOP 1

THE SLAVE TRADE CONSISTED OF THREE MAIN SEA VOYAGES TO THREE DIFFERENT LOCATIONS.

ON THE FIRST LEG OF THE JOURNEY, TRADING SHIPS SET OUT CARRYING THE SORT OF MANUFACTURED GOODS EUROPE SPECIALIZED IN—THINGS LIKE CLOTH, CUTLERY, RUM, AND ESPECIALLY GUNS. **LOTS** OF GUNS.

THE **PORTUGUESE** BEGAN THE TRANSATLANTIC SLAVE TRADE, BUT IT DIDN'T TAKE LONG FOR OTHER COUNTRIES TO GET IN ON THE ACT. PARTICULARLY **BRITAIN**, WHO BECAME THE INDUSTRY LEADER, ENSLAVING MORE AFRICANS THAN ANY OTHER NATION.

STOP 2: AFRICA

THE SHIPS TRADED THEIR GUNS TO AFRICAN COASTAL NATIONS LIKE THE **ASANTE**, **OYO**, AND **DAHOMENY**, WHO USED THEM TO DEFEAT THEIR ENEMIES AND TAKE THEM PRISONER.

THE VICTORS MARCHED THEIR CAPTIVES TO **SLAVE FORTS** ALONG THE COAST; CASTLES WHERE SLAVES WERE KEPT CHAINED UP UNTIL A SHIP CAME ALONG TO BUY THEM.

THEN BEGAN THE MOST HORRENDOUS PORTION OF THE WHOLE HORRIBLE BUSINESS, A TWO-MONTH-LONG OCEAN JOURNEY KNOWN AS "**THE MIDDLE PASSAGE**."

THE SLAVE TRADE, AND THE DAMAGE IT DID TO AFRICAN PEOPLE, REMAINS ONE OF THE MOST MASSIVE AND HORRIFIC ATROCITIES IN HUMAN HISTORY.

MEDICINE MAN, WAR CHIEF, VISIONARY, AS WELL AS THE LAST CHIEF OF THE GREAT SIOUX NATION TO LAY DOWN HIS RIFLE AND MAKE PEACE WITH THE UNITED STATES OF AMERICA...
PLEASE WELCOME THATHÁŊKA ÍYOTAKE, BETTER KNOWN AS...
SITTING BULL!
SITTING BULL
SIOUX LEADER
1831–1890

SITTING BULL, YOUR CRUSHING DEFEAT OF U.S. ARMY GENERAL GEORGE CUSTER AT THE BATTLE OF THE LITTLE BIGHORN WAS THE GREATEST SIOUX VICTORY IN THE WHOLE HISTORY OF THE WILD WEST.

WHICH IS ALL THE MORE IMPRESSIVE SINCE YOU WERE REALLY FAMOUS NOT AS A WAR CHIEF, BUT AS A MEDICINE MAN. IS THAT LIKE A DOCTOR?

HMM, NOT REALLY. A MEDICINE MAN OR WOMAN MIGHT DO SOME HEALING, BUT THE WORD WHITE PEOPLE TRANSLATED AS "MEDICINE" REALLY MEANS SOMETHING MORE LIKE "SACRED MYSTERY."

SO A **MEDICINE MAN** IS ONE WHO TRIES TO SPEAK WITH, AND TO UNDERSTAND, THE GREAT SACRED MYSTERY THAT CREATES AND PERMEATES THE WORLD.

SOUNDS... MYSTERIOUS...

YEAH, WELL, A LOT OF HOW WE THOUGHT DIDN'T MAKE MUCH SENSE TO WHITE PEOPLE.

AND VICE VERSA.

FOR EXAMPLE, AS SETTLERS MOVED INTO OUR COUNTRY, THEY STARTED FENCING OFF THE LAND WHERE OUR ANCESTORS HAD ONCE ROAMED FREELY.
THIS IS **MINE** NOW!

HOW CAN YOU SAY YOU **OWN** LAND—THE GIFT OF THE GREAT MYSTERY!? MIGHT AS WELL SAY YOU **OWN** THE SKY! HERE—THIS IS **MY** PART OF THE SKY! DON'T LOOK AT IT!

RIDICULOUS. BUT TO MAKE MATTERS WORSE, THE MASSIVE BUFFALO HERDS OF THE PLAINS WERE AN **INCONVENIENCE** TO THE SETTLERS AND THE NEWLY BUILT RAILROADS.

THEY ORGANIZED TRAIN-MOUNTED SHOOTING PARTIES TO KILL THE BUFFALO OFF. DIDN'T EVEN EAT THEM! JUST LEFT 'EM TO ROT!
WOO!
YEE-HAW!
BANG!
BANG!

THAT'S **INSANE**. THE GREAT MYSTERY CREATED THE WORLD FOR HUMANS AND ANIMALS TO LIVE IN **TOGETHER**! SURE, WE HUNTED BUFFALO, BUT ONLY FOR OUR **DINNER**.

WHICH IS ANOTHER GOOD POINT. WITHOUT THE BUFFALO WE HAD NOTHING TO **EAT**.

THE U.S. GOVERNMENT PROPOSED **RESERVING** SOME LAND ESPECIALLY FOR US, SO NO SETTLERS WOULD BE ALLOWED AND THEY'D PROVIDE US WITH FOOD TO MAKE UP FOR THE LOST BUFFALO.
HMM... NICE...?

OH **SURE**, WHY ROAM THE VAST **FREEDOM** OF THE GREAT PLAINS WHEN WE COULD LIVE **IMPRISONED** BEHIND FENCES AT THE MERCY OF WHITE MEN WHO **NEVER KEEP THEIR PROMISES**!

LIKE THE BLACK HILLS?

LIKE THE BLACK HILLS. OUR MOST HOLY PLACE. I MEAN, IT'S ONLY THE **SACRED CENTER** OF THE **WHOLE WORLD**!

THE GOVERNMENT PROMISED THAT, IF WE STAYED ON THE RESERVATIONS, THEY'D LEAVE THE BLACK HILLS ALONE. WHICH I DIDN'T BELIEVE FOR A **SECOND**.

TURNS OUT, THERE WAS **GOLD** IN THOSE HILLS. BEFORE YOU KNEW IT, THE WHOLE PLACE WAS **CRAWLING** WITH ILLEGAL, GREEDY GOLD-PROSPECTORS!

AND, INSTEAD OF KICKING THEM OUT, THE GOVERNMENT SENT AN ARMY TO PROTECT THEM AND **ARREST** US!

THEY DON'T STAND A CHANCE AGAINST A **MODERN** ARMY!

SOUNDS LIKE TROUBLE. WHAT DID YOU DO?

I CALLED A GATHERING OF THE TRIBES BESIDE THE **LITTLE BIGHORN RIVER**, AND PRAYED TO THE GREAT MYSTERY FOR GUIDANCE.

I CUT MY ARMS **100** TIMES AND DANCED, WITHOUT FOOD OR WATER, FOR DAYS, STARING INTO THE SUN, UNTIL I COLLAPSED.

WHOA. THAT'S QUITE A SERIOUS PRAYER...

YEAH, WELL, I **SERIOUSLY** NEEDED TO TALK TO THE GREAT MYSTERY.

IN MY TRANCE, I SAW A **VISION**. A TROOP OF SOLDIERS ON HORSEBACK, FALLING UPSIDE-DOWN INTO A VILLAGE OF TEPEES.

I TOOK IT TO BE A PREDICTION OF THE FUTURE. OUR BRAVES COULD GO INTO BATTLE **CERTAIN** THE ENEMY WOULD FALL, AS THE VISION FORETOLD.

AND WHEN CUSTER'S FORCES, CARELESS AND OVER-CONFIDENT, TRIED TO CHARGE YOUR ENCAMPMENT, THAT'S EXACTLY WHAT HAPPENED!

THE BATTLE OF THE LITTLE BIGHORN **UTTERLY OBLITERATED** A U.S. ARMY THAT THOUGHT ITSELF **UNBEATABLE**! HOW'D IT FEEL?

UM... NOT GREAT, ACTUALLY. THEY JUST SENT ANOTHER, BIGGER ARMY. I BEGAN TO REALIZE WE MIGHT'VE WON THE BATTLE, BUT WE COULDN'T WIN THE WAR.

STARVING TO DEATH, AND WITH NOWHERE TO GO, I DIDN'T NEED A **VISION** TO PREDICT THE ONLY WAY TO SAVE MY PEOPLE WAS TO SURRENDER...

WITH YOUR ARREST AND TRANSFER ONTO THE RESERVATIONS, AMERICA COULD FINALLY CONSIDER THE WEST TO BE WON.

BUT YOUR ADVENTURES WEREN'T QUITE OVER YET. BORED WITH LIVING OFF HANDOUTS ON THE RESERVATION, YOU BEGAN A BIZARRE SECOND CAREER AS A TOURIST ATTRACTION.

YEAH, I AGREED TO JOIN BUFFALO BILL'S WILD WEST SHOW, A SORT OF TRAVELING CIRCUS FEATURING FAMOUS PEOPLE FROM WHAT WAS NOW THE OLD WEST.
WILD WEST SHOW

ALL I HAD TO DO WAS WEAR MY WARBONNET AND RIDE AROUND A FEW TIMES (AND PUT UP WITH BEING BOOED AND HISSED AT).

I WAS SHOCKED BY WHAT THEY CALLED "CIVILIZATION." THE WHITE MAN'S VILLAGES HAD SO MANY PEOPLE IT MADE MY HEAD SPIN.

AND THEY HAD SO MUCH STUFF. BUT EVERYWHERE I WENT I SAW LOTS OF PEOPLE LIVING IN ABJECT POVERTY.

THEY CALLED US SAVAGES, BUT NO SIOUX WOULD LEAVE PEOPLE TO STARVE WHEN HE HAD FOOD TO GIVE THEM.

I ALWAYS SAID: "THE WHITE MAN KNOWS HOW TO MAKE EVERYTHING, BUT HE DOES NOT KNOW HOW TO DISTRIBUTE IT."

-AHEM-
SPEAKING OF WHICH...

COUNTING COUP

WE'VE JUST MET SITTING BULL, THE LAKOTA SIOUX CHIEF WHOSE VISIONARY LEADERSHIP INSPIRED THE LEGENDARY BATTLE OF THE LITTLE BIGHORN.

BUT I DIDN'T GET THE CHANCE TO ASK HIM ABOUT ONE OF THE MOST DISTINCTIVE AND RECOGNIZABLE TRADITIONS OF PLAINS TRIBES LIKE THE SIOUX, THE EAGLE-FEATHER WARBONNET.

THE COUP IS WHERE YOU JUST **TOUCH** AN ENEMY WITH YOUR HAND OR **COUP STICK** IN THE MIDDLE OF A BATTLE. SORT OF LIKE A GAME OF **TAG**, ONLY MORE DANGEROUS.

WHEN A YOUNG BRAVE COUNTS HIS FIRST COUP HE BECOMES A WARRIOR, AND IS PERMITTED TO WEAR A SINGLE EAGLE FEATHER TO COMMEMORATE THE ACHIEVEMENT.

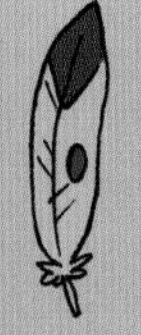

IN MY DAY, THE SIOUX WAS A WARRIOR SOCIETY. YOUNG MEN ACHIEVED SUCCESS AND RENOWN BY FIGHTING OTHER TRIBES, LIKE OUR OLD ENEMIES, THE CROW AND PAWNEE.

BUT KILLING A MAN IS ACTUALLY PRETTY EASY: YOU CAN JUST SHOOT HIM. WHERE'S THE HONOR IN THAT?

BY FAR THE **MOST** PRESTIGIOUS ACHIEVEMENT WAS THE **COUP** (PRONOUNCED "COO"— FROM THE FRENCH WORD FOR A BLOW OR STRIKE).

SOME OLD WARRIORS COUNTED SO MANY COUPS IN THEIR LIVES THEY NEEDED SOME SORT OF HEADGEAR TO WEAR THEM ALL. AND SO THE WARBONNET WAS BORN.

FEATHERS ARE SUPER IMPORTANT IN SIOUX SOCIETY BECAUSE THEY ALLOW THE WEARER TO TELL EVERYONE THE STORY OF HOW HE EARNED THEM. SO THEY WILL KNOW HOW TOTALLY AWESOME HE IS.

YOU COULD ALSO COUNT A COUP FOR OTHER ACTS OF DARING, LIKE STEALING A HORSE, DISARMING AN ENEMY, OR SAVING A FELLOW WARRIOR.

I COUNTED MY OWN FIRST COUP ON A RAID AGAINST THE CROW WHEN I WAS JUST **14**.

BY THE TIME I WAS AN OLD MAN, I HAD OVER **60** COUPS TO MY NAME.

MY NEXT GUEST IS ONE OF HISTORY'S MOST DE-VOTE-ED CAMPAIGNERS FOR WOMEN'S RIGHTS!
IT'S THE SPECTACULAR SUFFRAGETTE LEADER...
EMMELINE PANKHURST!
EMMELINE PANKHURST
SUFFRAGETTE LEADER
1858–1928

MRS PANKHURST, YOU DEDICATED YOUR LIFE TO WINNING THE RIGHT TO VOTE FOR WOMEN, WHY WAS THAT SO IMPORTANT?

WHY WAS IT SO...? YOUNG MAN! IT'S THE MOST IMPORTANT THING!

IN A DEMOCRACY, LIKE BRITAIN IS SUPPOSED TO BE, PEOPLE HAVE ONE WAY TO HAVE A SAY IN HOW THINGS ARE RUN, AND THAT IS TO VOTE.

IF YOU DON'T HAVE A VOTE, NO ONE NEEDS TO LISTEN TO **ANYTHING** YOU SAY. THAT MEANS YOU ARE NOT A **PERSON**—YOU ARE **PROPERTY**.

WOMEN IN BRITAIN HAD BEEN TRYING FOR **YEARS** TO GET THE VOTE, BUT SINCE THEY DIDN'T **HAVE** THE VOTE, THE GOVERNMENT DIDN'T NEED TO LISTEN TO THEM.

"DEAR PRIME MINISTER, WOMEN THINK THAT..."
HA HA HA HA!

SO, ALONG WITH MY DAUGHTERS, I FOUNDED A NEW, RADICAL ORGANIZATION DETERMINED TO DO **WHATEVER IT TOOK** TO WIN WOMEN'S **SUFFRAGE** (THE RIGHT TO VOTE).

WE NAMED OURSELVES THE **WOMEN'S SOCIAL AND POLITICAL UNION**, BUT BEFORE LONG EVERYONE JUST CALLED US **SUFFRAGETTES**.

IT WAS SUPPOSED TO BE A DEMEANING NICKNAME, BUT WE QUICKLY REALIZED IT WAS **WAY CATCHIER**.

I MEAN, COME ON! WOMEN'S SOCIAL AND POLITICAL UNION? WHAT A MOUTHFUL!

I TOOK TO THE ROAD TO WHIP UP SUPPORT FOR OUR NEW PLAN OF DIRECT-ACTION PROTEST TACTICS.

SISTERS! THE GOVERNMENT REFUSES TO LISTEN! THE TIME FOR WORDS IS OVER! NOW IS THE TIME FOR **DEEDS**!

HEAR HEAR!
HURRAH!

WE STARTED BY BREAKING WINDOWS, LIKE THE PRIME MINISTER'S AT 10 DOWNING STREET.

I USED TO SAY THAT "THE BROKEN WINDOW IS THE MOST PERSUASIVE ARGUMENT IN MODERN POLITICS."

WE CHAINED OURSELVES TO THE RAILINGS OUTSIDE PARLIAMENT.

HOW EMBARRASSING!

FOR **THEM**! THEY COULDN'T IGNORE US, THEN!

FROM THERE, WE HIT THEM WHERE IT **REALLY** HURTS. ON THE **GOLF COURSE**!
BURNED WITH ACID
VOTES FOR WOMEN

OH, AND PUNCHING POLICEMEN. I ALWAYS LIKED THAT...
BIFF!

NOT **HARD**, YOU KNOW... JUST SO WE'D GET ARRESTED.

YOU **WANTED** TO GET ARRESTED?

WE WANTED TO SHOW THAT WE WERE NOT PREPARED TO BE GOVERNED BY LAWS ON WHICH WE WERE NOT CONSULTED.

SO THEY PUT US IN JAIL. I MYSELF WAS ARRESTED SEVEN OR EIGHT TIMES.

THEY THOUGHT THAT WOULD SHUT US UP! BUT WE CONTINUED TO FIGHT IN THE ONLY WAY LEFT TO US—**HUNGER STRIKE**!

IT WOULD HAVE LOOKED BAD IF SUFFRAGETTES STARTED **DYING** IN PRISON, SO THE GOVERNMENT RELEASED US...
HUNGRY, MRS. PANKHURST?
OH, I COULD EAT A HORSE.

ONLY TO ARREST US AGAIN AS SOON AS WE HAD RECOVERED.
FEELING BETTER, MRS. PANKHURST?
-COFF- STILL VERY WEAK, OFFICER...

ALL OF WHICH MADE IT MOST INCONVENIENT FOR ME TO GIVE SPEECHES, SINCE NOW THE POLICE WERE WAITING WHEREVER I WENT.
OK, **NOW** YOU'RE BETTER...

I HAD TO RELY ON MY JIU-JITSU-TRAINED SUFFRAGETTE BODYGUARDS TO KEEP THEM AT BAY.

HOLD ON, DID YOU JUST SAY **JIU-JITSU-TRAINED SUFFRAGETTE BODYGUARDS!?**

WELL, AS OUR NOTORIETY GREW, THE POLICE, AND EVEN ANGRY MEMBERS OF THE PUBLIC, BEGAN TO GET REALLY QUITE VIOLENT.

SO I ENCOURAGED ALL SUFFRAGETTES TO LEARN SELF-DEFENSE, EVEN RECRUITING ONE OF BRITAIN'S FIRST WOMEN MARTIAL ARTISTS, **EDITH GARRUD**, TO TRAIN THEM.

JIU-JITSU, A JAPANESE UNARMED COMBAT SYSTEM, WAS IDEAL FOR WOMEN, SINCE IT SPECIALIZES IN USING AN OPPONENT'S STRENGTH AGAINST THEM.

WE DIDN'T START THIS FIGHT. BUT WE WERE READY TO DO **ANYTHING** TO END IT.

ALMOST ANYTHING.
WELL YES, IN **1914** WORLD WAR I BROKE OUT, AND THAT CHANGED THINGS...

THE THREAT WAS **SO GREAT**, THAT I CALLED FOR A TOTAL SUSPENSION OF SUFFRAGETTE ACTIVITY, SO EVERYONE COULD PULL TOGETHER TO WIN THE WAR.

WITH ALL THE MEN AWAY FIGHTING, WOMEN HAD TO DO THE JOBS THEY'D LEFT BEHIND.

SO IN THE END IT WAS A **COMBINATION** OF THE SUFFRAGETTES, THE WAR, AND JUST THE CHANGING TIMES...

BUT EITHER WAY, WOMEN DID FINALLY GET THE RIGHT TO VOTE.
AND I'M SURE ALL THE WOMEN OF BRITAIN WOULD OFFER YOU A **VOTE** OF **THANKS**!

NO JOB FOR A LADY?

SOCIETY-SHAPING SUFFRAGETTE **EMMELINE PANKHURST** SAW THE ROLE OF WOMEN RADICALLY REVISED BY THE ONSET OF **WORLD WAR I**.

THE WAR CHANGED **EVERYTHING**.

HOW COULD IT **NOT**, WHEN SO MANY MEN WERE AWAY, AND SO MANY NEVER CAME BACK?

WITH MILLIONS OF JOBS **LEFT EMPTY** BY THE MEN WHO'D GONE TO FIGHT, THERE WAS REALLY NO **OPTION** BUT TO LET WOMEN DO THEM.

ALMOST A **MILLION** WOMEN WENT INTO **MUNITIONS FACTORIES**, PRODUCING VAST QUANTITIES OF GUNS, PLANES, BOMBS, AND BULLETS.

MUNITIONETTES WERE RELATIVELY WELL PAID, BUT THE WORK WAS UNPLEASANT AND DANGEROUS.

TNT EXPLOSIVES ARE **LETHALLY TOXIC**, NOT TO MENTION ALL THE **POISON GAS** THE ARMY USED BACK THEN.

AND OF COURSE, EXPLOSIVES **EXPLODE**. SEVERAL MUNITIONS FACTORIES WENT UP IN SMOKE, TAKING THEIR MUNITIONETTES WITH THEM.

A QUARTER OF A MILLION WOMEN VOLUNTEERED FOR THE **WOMEN'S LAND ARMY**, AND WERE HIRED OUT AS CHEAP LABOR TO FARMERS.

FARMERETTES (YES, THEY REALLY LIKED THE -ETTE SUFFIX BACK THEN) BASICALLY **REPLACED** FARM MACHINERY, LIKE TRACTORS, SO THE ARMY COULD USE THE **FUEL**.

THE FIRST WOMEN **POLICE OFFICERS** WERE EMPLOYED DURING **WWI** AS WERE THE FIRST FIREFIGHTERS, BUS DRIVERS, TICKET COLLECTORS, AND POSTAL WORKERS.

GO ON, PAL. CALL ME "OFFICERETTE"—I DARE YA...

MORE THAN **100,000** JOINED THE **WOMEN'S ARMY AUXILIARY CORPS**, AND ITS SISTER BRANCHES IN THE NAVY AND AIR FORCE. THEY TOOK OVER NONCOMBAT ARMY JOBS LIKE COOKING, DRIVING, MECHANIC DUTIES, AND OFFICE WORK, FREEING UP MORE MEN TO FIGHT.

DURING THE WAR, IT WAS ALL ABOUT WOMEN DOING **WHATEVER IT TOOK** FOR THEIR COUNTRY.

BUT IT WAS A DIFFERENT STORY WHEN THE WAR ENDED...

THE MEN COMING HOME WERE AFRAID THEY'D BEEN REPLACED.

BUT THEY NEEDN'T HAVE WORRIED. IN MOST CASES, WOMEN WERE UNCEREMONIOUSLY KICKED OUT AND WERE TOLD TO GO HOME.

BUT THEIR SACIFICE, DEDICATION, AND OBVIOUS COMPETENCE IN THE WORKFORCE DIDN'T GO **ENTIRELY** UNREWARDED...
THE GOVERNMENT FINALLY GAVE WOMEN THE RIGHT TO VOTE IN **1918**, JUST AFTER THE WAR ENDED.
WELL... RICH WOMEN OVER **30** GOT IT IN **1918**. EVERYONE ELSE HAD TO WAIT ANOTHER **10** YEARS. BUT THEY GOT IT EVENTUALLY...

MY NEXT GUEST IS THE MAN WHO TOOK ON THE BRITISH EMPIRE **AND WON!** AND TO DO IT, HE DEVELOPED A NEW AND **RATHER SURPRISING** WEAPON...
PLEASE WELCOME THE FABULOUS **FATHER OF INDIA...**
MOHANDAS "MAHATMA" GANDHI!
MOHANDAS GANDHI
INDIAN ACTIVIST
1869–1948

GANDHI, AS A SMALL BOY IN INDIA, COULD YOU HAVE EVER IMAGINED THAT YOU WOULD GROW UP TO BE ONE OF THE GREATEST **FREEDOM FIGHTERS** OF ALL TIME?

NO, I DON'T THINK SO. I WAS A VERY **SHY** LITTLE BOY—NOT THE SORT YOU MIGHT EXPECT TO BECOME A GREAT LEADER!

I USED TO RUN HOME FROM SCHOOL TO AVOID GETTING PICKED ON.

WHEN I FIRST MET MY WIFE (OUR PARENTS ARRANGED IT WHEN I WAS 13) I WAS TOO SHY TO SPEAK TO HER.

I BECAME A LAWYER, BUT AT MY FIRST CASE, I WAS TOO SHY TO SPEAK IN COURT!

I HAD TO GIVE MY CLIENTS THEIR MONEY BACK AND TELL THEM TO FIND ANOTHER LAWYER!

SO HOW DID YOU FINALLY GET OVER YOUR SHYNESS?

WELL, I TOOK A JOB IN **SOUTH AFRICA**, WHICH MEANT I COULD JUST DO PAPERWORK WITHOUT HAVING TO TALK TO ANYONE...
OR SO I THOUGHT...

I'D ONLY BEEN THERE A WEEK, WHEN I GOT THROWN OFF A TRAIN JUST FOR BEING INDIAN!
CAN'T YOU READ? GET OFF!

THAT MADE ME SO **MAD** THAT I **COULDN'T** KEEP QUIET!
MY FELLOW INDIANS! THIS IS RIDICULOUS!
YEAH, BUT WHAT ARE WE GOING TO DO ABOUT IT?

WHAT **COULD** WE DO!? WE WERE FEW, POOR, AND WE HAD NO WEAPONS. WE COULDN'T FIGHT BACK!

BUT YOU HAD A **SECRET WEAPON**!

IT'S THE **STRONGEST** WEAPON OF ALL! ONE THAT ALWAYS WINS IN THE END...

...LOVE!

WITH LOVE YOU CAN FORGIVE YOUR ENEMIES. LIKE ONE TIME I WAS ATTACKED BY A MOB FOR SPEAKING OUT FOR THE INDIAN PEOPLE.

BUT I REFUSED TO HAVE THEM ARRESTED FOR IT.
HE WHAT!?
PHEW! I WAS WORRIED THERE...
Y'KNOW, MAYBE HE'S NOT SUCH A BAD GUY AFTER ALL...

AND **THAT'S** HOW YOU WIN OVER YOUR ENEMIES AND MAKE THEM YOUR FRIENDS!

YOU RETURNED TO INDIA, DETERMINED TO USE YOUR NEW WEAPON TO MAKE PEOPLE'S LIVES BETTER THERE, TOO!

INDIA WAS PART OF THE BRITISH EMPIRE, AND THE BRITISH HAD ALL SORTS OF WAYS TO GET RICH AT OUR EXPENSE.

HO HO
MAN...

THAT'S WHEN I STARTED WEARING THE **DHOTI**.
THE WHAT?
THIS TRADITIONAL GARMENT THAT INDIANS HAVE BEEN WEARING FOR CENTURIES.

INSTEAD OF BUYING EXPENSIVE BRITISH CLOTHES, WE COULD JUST MAKE OUR OWN! I ALWAYS LED BY EXAMPLE, SO THAT'S WHAT I DID!

BUT JUST CHANGING YOUR CLOTHES WASN'T GOING TO GET THE BRITISH OUT OF INDIA! IT WASN'T TIME TO BRING OUT THE **BIG GUNS**...
NONCOOPERATION!

IF A LAW WAS EVIL AND WRONG, WE'D JUST REFUSE TO FOLLOW IT!

BUT IF YOU BROKE THE LAW, DIDN'T YOU GET PUT IN JAIL?

ALL THE TIME!

SOON, THERE WERE **SO MANY** PEOPLE IN JAIL THAT THEY RAN OUT OF ROOM!

AND OF COURSE, THEY COULD BEAT US AND KILL US, BUT LOVE IS STRONGER THAN FEAR!

PICTURE IT! THOUSANDS OF PEOPLE LINING UP FEARLESSLY TO BE BEATEN.

THIS IS CRUEL AND RIDICULOUS!
UH, YEAH, YOU HAVE A POINT...

THE WORLD WAS HORRIFIED! BRITAIN WAS HORRIFIED! THEY THOUGHT THE BRITISH WERE CIVILIZED...

BUT HERE THEY WERE, BEATING AND KILLING FRIENDLY, UNARMED, DEFENSELESS PEOPLE!

I'M EMBARRASSED.
MAKES ONE ASHAMED TO BE BRITISH!
NOT CRICKET, WHAT?

ALTHOUGH IT TOOK ANOTHER TWELVE YEARS, IT WAS AT THAT MOMENT I KNEW THE BRITISH WOULD LEAVE INDIA.

BUT DOES IT REALLY WORK!? EVEN AFTER ALL YOU HAVE TAUGHT, PEOPLE ARE STILL FIGHTING AND KILLING ONE ANOTHER!

YOU WERE SHOT DEAD BY A YOUNG MAN WHO WAS ANGRY THAT YOU DIDN'T HATE MUSLIMS.

WILL LOVE REALLY WIN IN THE END!? WILL WE EVER LEARN TO LIVE IN PEACE!?

WILL WE!? WILL WE REALLY, GANDHI!?
THERE, THERE.
UH... YOU'RE GETTING ME WET...

THE ART OF NONVIOLENCE

MOHANDAS "MAHATMA" GANDHI'S PRINCIPLES OF NONVIOLENT RESISTANCE HAVE INSPIRED LEADERS LIKE DR. MARTIN LUTHER KING JR., NELSON MANDELA, AND MANY, MANY OTHERS.
BUT WHAT IS "NONVIOLENT RESISTANCE"?
THE BASIC PRINCIPLE BEHIND NONVIOLENCE IS THIS: ALL LIFE IS ONE.
SOUNDS LIKE SOME GRAND, COSMIC PROCLAMATION, RIGHT?
AND INDEED IT IS. BUT IT'S ALSO VERY PRACTICAL AND EVERYDAY.
PUBLIC LIBRARY
EVERYTHING GOOD IN OUR LIVES COMES FROM A WEB OF INTERCONNECTED KINDNESS, OF PEOPLE DOING THINGS IN THE HOPE OF HELPING OTHERS.
NONVIOLENCE IS JUST THE PRINCIPLED APPLICATION OF THAT IDEA IN THE FACE OF HATRED AND INJUSTICE.

NONVIOLENCE IS **NOT** DOING NOTHING. IT MEANS ACTIVELY SPEAKING **AND ACTING ON** THE TRUTH, WHATEVER THE CONSEQUENCES.

THIS IS NOT A PATH FOR COWARDS—IT CALLS FOR PROFOUND COURAGE, OFTEN IN THE FACE OF VERY REAL DANGER.

THE GOAL IS **NOT** TO DEFEAT OR HUMILIATE PEOPLE, BUT TO AWAKEN THEIR **INNATE GOODNESS**.

REMEMBER, WE ARE FIGHTING EVIL **FORCES** IN SOCIETY, NOT EVIL **PEOPLE**.

SOME PEOPLE SEEM TO BENEFIT FROM INJUSTICE, TO SUPPORT OR EVEN ENACT IT. BUT IT HURTS THEM TOO, SINCE WE ARE ALL CONNECTED.

NONVIOLENCE MEANS BEING READY TO ACCEPT HATRED, VIOLENCE, OR IMPRISONMENT **WITHOUT** RETALIATION.
IT HELPS TO REMEMBER THAT **SUFFERING ITSELF** IS POWERFUL. MANY OF THE MOST IMPORTANT LESSONS IN LIFE CAN ONLY BE LEARNED BY COURAGE IN THE FACE OF SUFFERING.
POL
WE REFUSE NOT ONLY TO **HURT** OTHERS, BUT ALSO TO **HATE, INSULT**, OR EVEN **THINK BADLY** OF THEM.
NONVIOLENCE IS NOT JUST THE ACTIONS WE PERFORM, IT IS THE **SPIRIT** BEHIND THOSE ACTIONS.
WE DRAW HOPE FROM THE BELIEF THAT **THE UNIVERSE** IS ON THE SIDE OF JUSTICE.
HISTORY RECORDS LOTS OF WARS, BUT **MUCH MORE COMMON** ARE EVERYDAY ACTS OF LOVE AND COOPERATION.
WE LIVE IN A UNIQUELY DANGEROUS TIME.
OUR WEAPONS ARE MORE POWERFUL THAN EVER, AND OUR SOCIETY ACTIVELY PROMOTES GREED, CONSUMPTION, AND DOG-EAT-DOG COMPETITION.
HISTORY IS NOT A STRAIGHT LINE, NOR IS THE OUTCOME CERTAIN.
BUT, IT **IS** CLEARLY THE STORY OF PEOPLE TRYING TO BUILD BETTER, KINDER, MORE JUST SOCIETIES.
AND ALL OF US CAN BE A PART OF THAT.
AS I LIKED TO SAY: "**BE** THE DIFFERENCE YOU WANT TO SEE IN THE WORLD."

MY NEXT GUEST IS A DIFFERENT SORT OF REBEL: A FEARLESS FREE SPIRIT WHOSE LIFE IS AS REVOLUTIONARY AS HER ART!
PLEASE MAKE SOME NOISE FOR ONE OF THE MOST RESPECTED ARTISTS IN MODERN ART...
FRIDA KAHLO!
FRIDA KAHLO
MEXICAN ARTIST
1907–1954

FRIDA, YOU ARE TODAY THE WORLD'S MOST FAMOUS AND SUCCESSFUL FEMALE PAINTER. BUT YOU DIDN'T PLAN ON GOING INTO ART AT ALL...

I DIDN'T PLAN ON A LOT OF THINGS, MY FRIEND. BUT LIFE DOESN'T ALWAYS FOLLOW YOUR PLANS.

I WAS PLANNING ON BECOMING A DOCTOR...

BUT THEN THE BUS I WAS RIDING COLLIDED WITH AN ELECTRIC TROLLEY-CAR.

BROKEN SPINAL COLUMN, BROKEN COLLARBONE, BROKEN RIBS, SHATTERED PELVIS, 11 FRACTURES IN RIGHT LEG, CRUSHED RIGHT FOOT...

IT WAS **MONTHS** BEFORE I COULD EVEN GET OUT OF BED. MY PARENTS BOUGHT ME A PAINTING SET TO KEEP ME OCCUPIED.

PAINTING BECAME MY **SANCTUARY**. AND SINCE I SPENT SO MUCH TIME ALONE, I PAINTED WHAT I KNEW BEST—MYSELF.

YOU ALSO MADE THE, ER... **UNUSUAL** DECISION TO PAINT YOURSELF WITH THE... UH...
THE **WHAT**? THE **MUSTACHE**!? THE **MONOBROW**!? YOU'RE HARDLY ONE TO TALK!
POINT TAKEN.
ANYWAY, WHAT DO I CARE WHAT SOME IDIOTS THINK? I LOOK THE WAY I LOOK.

AND IT WAS YOUR FEARLESS HONESTY THAT CAUGHT THE EYE OF MEXICO'S MOST FAMOUS ARTIST, THE MURALIST **DIEGO RIVERA**.

YES, DIEGO! I LOVED HIM SO TERRIBLY MUCH!
UH... **THAT** GUY?

OK, MAYBE HE DOESN'T SEEM LIKE YOUR CUP OF TEA, BUT HE WAS THE GREAT ARTISTIC HERO OF MEXICO. WOMEN **LOVED** HIM.

ACTUALLY, THAT WAS KIND OF THE PROBLEM. WE GOT MARRIED, BUT HE WOULDN'T STOP CHASING OTHER WOMEN.

OH SURE, I LAUGHED, I JOKED, I ACTED LIKE IT WASN'T A BIG DEAL.

BUT IT HURT.

I USED TO SAY, THERE WERE **TWO** ACCIDENTS IN MY LIFE; THE TROLLEY-CAR AND DIEGO, AND DIEGO WAS THE WORST.

NOW **ALL MY LIFE** WAS PAIN. PAIN IN MY SHATTERED BODY, AND PAIN IN MY BROKEN HEART.

I TRIED DRINKING TO DROWN MY SORROWS, BUT THE DAMN THINGS LEARNED TO SWIM!

ONLY ONE THING HELPED. **PAINTING**.

IF I WAS SPLIT IN TWO BY HEARTBREAK...

OR TORN TO PIECES BY MISCARRIAGES AND UNSUCCESSFUL SURGERIES...

NO MATTER HOW TERRIBLE THE PAIN, IF I COULD PAINT IT, I COULD ENDURE IT.

YOUR SUCCESS GREW AND GREW, AS YOUR HONESTY AND PASSION INSPIRED PEOPLE AROUND THE WORLD.

BUT YOUR HEALTH GOT WORSE AND WORSE UNTIL, DESPITE MORE THAN 30 OPERATIONS, YOU WERE UNABLE TO EVEN GET OUT OF BED.

WHICH IS KIND OF A PROBLEM IF YOU HAVE A MASSIVE EXHIBITION OPENING AND YOU CAN'T GO TO YOUR OWN PARTY!

WELL, I WASN'T GOING TO LET SOMETHING LIKE THAT STOP ME!
KNOCK!
KNOCK!

SO I WENT IN MY PAJAMAS!

YOU MADE A BED-DAZZLING ENTRANCE!
¡DIOS MIO!

ALL RIGHT, LISTEN UP! THIS HERE IS...
SELF-PORTRAITS WITH FRIDA KAHLO!
SELF-PORTRAIT JUST MEANS PAINTING YOURSELF.
BUT NOT JUST PAINTING WHAT YOU LOOK LIKE, BUT WHO YOU ARE ON THE INSIDE!
WE'RE NOT HERE TO PAINT PRETTY PICTURES. THIS IS ABOUT TRUE REALITY!
OK. HERE'S HOW I DO IT. FIRST, GRAB A MIRROR.
WHAT IS MOST DISTINCTIVE ABOUT HOW YOU LOOK? LIKE, I DON'T KNOW... A MONOBROW OR A MUSTACHE...
GIANT FOREHEAD?
GAP TEETH?
EVERYBODY HAS SOMETHING.
WHO CARES! LET'S PAINT 'EM ANYWAY!
BUT THAT'S JUST THE BEGINNING...
NOW YOU'VE PAINTED HOW YOU LOOK, BUT HOW DO YOU FEEL?
WHAT ARE THE GREAT SORROWS OF YOUR LIFE!?
FEELING TORN APART BY PAIN?
PAINT IT!

BURIED ALIVE BY WORRIES?
PAINT 'EM!
MAYBE YOU JUST FEEL SAD ALL THE TIME?
PAINT IT ALL! BE BRAVE! BE FEARLESS!
THIS IS YOUR TRUTH!
THE TRUTH OF HOW YOU FEEL, WHICH ONLY YOU CAN KNOW, IS ONE OF THE TRUEST THINGS YOU CAN KNOW.
YOU CAN ALSO PAINT SOME OF YOUR GREAT LOVES!
LIFE IS STILL WONDERFUL, AFTER ALL...
PETS!
PEOPLE YOU CARE ABOUT!
BIRDS SINGING IN THE SUNSHINE!
FEEL FREE TO USE LOTS OF BRIGHT COLORS!
FOR EXTRA BONUS FRIDA POINTS, TRY MIXING THE HAPPY AND SAD THINGS IN THE SAME PAINTING!
GENIUS! YOU'RE ALL MASTERPIECES!
PAINT IT ALL!
WELL, MY WORK HERE IS DONE!

MY NEXT GUEST IS ONE OF THE MOST FAMOUS, FARSIGHTED AND FREQUENTLY PARAPHRASED FREEDOM FIGHTERS OF ALL TIME!
IT'S THE SUPERB SPOKESMAN OF THE SOUTHERN CIVIL RIGHTS CAMPAIGN...
DR. MARTIN LUTHER KING JR.!
DR. MARTIN LUTHER KING JR.
MINISTER & ACTIVIST
1929–1968
DR. KING, YOU DEVOTED YOUR LIFE TO FIGHTING FOR THE RIGHTS OF BLACK PEOPLE IN AMERICA. WHAT STARTED YOU ON YOUR QUEST FOR JUSTICE?
WELL, LOTS OF THINGS...
BUT THE FIRST I REMEMBER WAS THE KID WHO'D BEEN MY BEST FRIEND SAYING, "MY DAD DOESN'T WANT ME TO BE FRIENDS WITH YOU ANY MORE."
BECAUSE YOU WERE BLACK? THAT'S RIDICULOUS!
WELL, YES, EXACTLY. BUT THE THING IS—THE WHOLE SOCIETY WAS LIKE THAT.

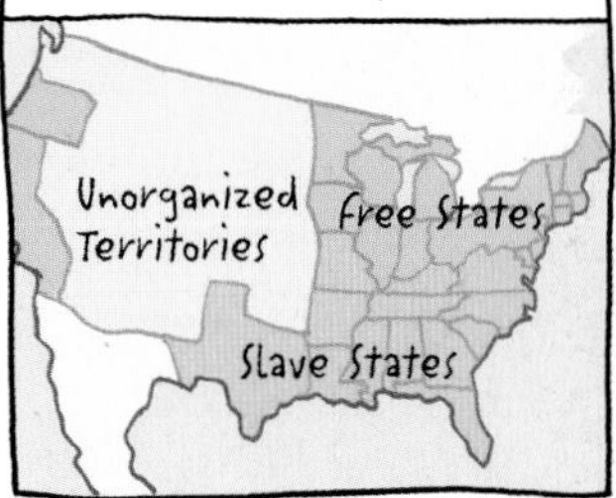
AFTER THEY LOST THE AMERICAN CIVIL WAR, SOUTHERN STATES WERE **FORCED** INTO ABOLISHING (OFFICIALLY ENDING) SLAVERY.
Unorganized Territories
Free States
Slave States

BUT FREEDOM FROM SLAVERY WASN'T ACTUALLY **REAL**, BECAUSE THOSE STATES HAD DEVELOPED A COMPLEX SET OF LOCAL LAWS AND UNWRITTEN CUSTOMS DESIGNED TO KEEP BLACK PEOPLE AS **CLOSE** TO SLAVERY AS THEY COULD.

WE COULDN'T SIT NEXT TO WHITE PEOPLE, COULDN'T SHARE A MEAL WITH THEM, COULDN'T SHAKE HANDS WITH THEM, COULDN'T CALL WHITE PEOPLE BY THEIR FIRST NAME...

HECK, WE COULDN'T EVEN PEE IN THE SAME **TOILET BOWL**! AND IF THEY **DID** PROVIDE FACILITIES FOR BLACK PEOPLE, THEY WERE ALWAYS **TERRIBLE**.
WOMEN
MEN
COLORED

NOT JUST TOILETS EITHER, BUT SCHOOLS, LIBRARIES, HOUSES, JOBS, HEALTHCARE. LITERALLY EVERYTHING YOU COULD THINK OF, OURS WERE WORSE.

AND THERE WERE GANGS OF **TERRORISTS** GOING AROUND BEATING, SHOOTING, AND KILLING BLACK PEOPLE FOR THE **TINIEST** BREACH OF THEIR RULES.

I WAS LUCKY—I NEVER EXPERIENCED THAT FIRSTHAND. BUT I REMEMBER SEEING THE BODIES, WHEN I WAS A LITTLE KID.
GOOD GRIEF.

THAT WAS ACTUALLY ONE OF THE MOST EFFECTIVE TOOLS THEY HAD—THE CONSTANT FEAR, AND THE KNOWLEDGE THAT NO ONE WOULD HELP, KEPT US FROM REALIZING WE **COULD** STAND UP TO IT.

THAT'S **TERRIBLE**...
BUT YOU KNOW WHAT **REALLY** GOT TO ME?

IT WAS THE LITTLE THINGS...

THE CONSTANT, DAILY REMINDERS THAT WE WEREN'T AS VALUED, RESPECTED, OR REALLY EVEN CONSIDERED AS **HUMAN** AS WHITE PEOPLE.
WHITE ONLY

I REMEMBER ONE TIME, I WON A HIGH SCHOOL DEBATING CONTEST...
CONGRATS.
OH, THANKS.

I WAS PRETTY PROUD OF IT. MY WINNING SPEECH WAS ABOUT HOW THE U.S. DECLARATION OF INDEPENDENCE SAYS "ALL MEN ARE CREATED EQUAL" AND HOW IT STILL DIDN'T APPLY TO US.

BUT ON THE WAY HOME, I **STILL** HAD TO GIVE UP MY SEAT WHEN WHITE PASSENGERS GOT ON.

I WAS GOING TO REFUSE, BUT MY TEACHER REMINDED ME IT WAS THE **LAW**. I WOULD'VE GOTTEN ARRESTED. HER TOO, PROBABLY.

I STOOD IN THE AISLE ALL THE WAY HOME. THAT WAS THE **ANGRIEST** I EVER WAS IN MY **LIFE**.

BUT YOU KNOW WHAT INFURIATED ME? MOST WHITE PEOPLE DIDN'T REALLY **NOTICE**! TO THEM IT WAS ALL JUST **NATURAL**.

AFTER ALL, THEY'D BEEN TAUGHT THEIR WHOLE LIVES THAT THEY WERE JUST **MORE IMPORTANT** THAN US.

you're worth it!

AFTER A WHILE, I STOPPED HATING THEM AND STARTED TO **PITY** THEM INSTEAD.

AND FROM PITYING THEM, I CAME TO LOVE AND **FORGIVE** THEM.

REALLY? YOU COULD **FORGIVE** ALL THAT!?

FORGIVENESS DOESN'T MEAN **PUTTING UP** WITH OTHERS' EVIL THOUGHTS OR ACTIONS.

BUT IT **DOES** MEAN MAKING A DISTINCTION BETWEEN EVIL **ACTIONS** AND EVIL **PEOPLE**. EVEN THE BEST PEOPLE HAVE FAULTS, AND I THINK EVEN THE WORST PEOPLE DESERVE A FRESH START, **IF** THEY CHOOSE TO TAKE IT.

SO WHAT CHANGED?

WELL, FIRST OFF, RACISM ISN'T THE ONLY FORM OF INJUSTICE.

I REALIZED THAT POOR WHITE PEOPLE WERE BEING TAKEN ADVANTAGE OF TOO, BY RICH BUSINESS OWNERS AND POLITICIANS.

IT'S ALL TOO EASY FOR THE PEOPLE IN POWER TO MAKE LAWS THAT HELP THEMSELVES, AND HURT EVERYBODY ELSE.
OK, HEAR ME OUT ON THIS. HOW ABOUT A MASSIVE TAX CUT... FOR US!

THE OTHER THING WAS THE CHURCH. I HAD A LOT OF PROBLEMS WITH THE CHURCH, LORD KNOWS, BUT AT THE HEART OF JESUS' TEACHINGS I FOUND THIS WONDERFUL MESSAGE OF LOVE AND FORGIVENESS.

HATE ROTS THE SOUL, BUT LOVE MADE ME FEEL WHOLE AGAIN. I DECIDED TO BECOME A MINISTER, TO SHARE THAT MESSAGE OF LOVE.

AND IT WAS WHILE I WAS TRAINING AS A MINISTER THAT I FIRST HEARD OF THIS AMAZING GUY NAMED GANDHI—MAYBE YOU'VE HEARD OF HIM?
THE, UM... THE NAME RINGS A BELL...

GANDHI USED LOVE AND FORGIVENESS LIKE A WEAPON, AND HAD COMPLETELY OVERTURNED THE BRITISH EMPIRE IN INDIA.

ONE OF HIS CORE STRATEGIES WAS CIVIL DISOBEDIENCE, THE TARGETED BREAKING OF UNJUST LAWS TO GRIND SOCIETY TO A HALT AND FORCE IT TO CONFRONT INJUSTICE.

I THOUGHT A SIMILAR STRATEGY MIGHT WORK IN AMERICA, AND BEGAN BUILDING A NETWORK OF LIKE-MINDED RELIGIOUS MINISTERS AND CIVIL RIGHTS ACTIVISTS.

BUT WE NEEDED A CAUSE, A SINGLE INCIDENT SO UNJUST, WE COULD BUILD IT INTO SOMETHING UNAVOIDABLE.

AND THEN ROSA PARKS, A COURAGEOUS ACTIVIST FROM MONTGOMERY, ALABAMA, DECIDED NOT TO GIVE UP HER BUS SEAT, AND GOT ARRESTED.

SHE SAID LATER, SHE DIDN'T MEAN TO START A MASSIVE PROTEST. SHE JUST COULDN'T TAKE THE INDIGNITY ANY MORE.

BUT HER DEFIANT ACT WOULD GO ON TO HAVE A PROFOUND EFFECT, PROVIDING THE INCIDENT THAT SPARKED THE CIVIL RIGHTS MOVEMENT!

THE LOCAL ACTIVISTS CALLED A BOYCOTT OF THE MONTGOMERY BUS COMPANY, AND THEY ASKED ME TO LEAD IT!

UNTIL THE LAW WAS CHANGED TO TREAT US FAIRLY, NO BLACK PERSON WOULD TAKE THE BUS!
HOW DID YOU GET AROUND?

WE WALKED. WE CARPOOLED— SOME PEOPLE EVEN GOT OUT THEIR OLD HORSE-DRAWN CARTS.

BLACK PEOPLE WERE THE MAJORITY OF BUS CUSTOMERS. SO THE BUS COMPANY WAS GOING BANKRUPT, SINCE NO ONE WAS BUYING TICKETS.

BUT THE BOYCOTTERS WERE LOSING MONEY TOO, FROM BEING LATE TO WORK OR GETTING FIRED...

BLACK CHURCHES ALL OVER AMERICA COLLECTED OLD SHOES TO SEND TO BOYCOTTERS WHO WERE WEARING OUT THEIR SOLES WITH ALL THAT WALKING!

BUT LOCAL TERRORISTS TRIED TO INTIMIDATE THE BOYCOTTERS, ATTACKING BLACK PEOPLE WALKING TO WORK.

IT ALL CAME DOWN TO WHICH SIDE WOULD GIVE UP FIRST! PART OF MY JOB WAS TO ENCOURAGE AND INSPIRE THE BOYCOTTERS, AS WELL AS EXPLAINING OUR GOALS TO THE WIDER WORLD.

AND YOU KNOW WHAT, WE WERE WINNING! OUR CAMPAIGN GOT MASSIVE NATIONAL NEWS COVERAGE THAT TURNED THE TIDE OF PUBLIC OPINION.

ROSA PARKS' CASE GOT BUMPED UP TO A FEDERAL COURT, WHICH RULED THAT THE SEPARATE BUS SEATS THING WAS UNCONSTITUTIONAL (AND THEREFORE ILLEGAL).

AFTER 381 GRUELING DAYS, THE BUS COMPANY WAS FORCED TO ABANDON SEGREGATION AND LET PEOPLE SIT WHERE THEY LIKED!

SOUNDS LIKE THE BOYCOTT WORKED...

WELL, YES AND NO. I MEAN, WE WON. BUT A LOT OF PEOPLE WERE NOT HAPPY ABOUT IT...

THE TERRORISTS RAMPED UP THEIR VIOLENT CAMPAIGN, SHOOTING INTO BUSES AND BLOWING UP CHURCHES.
MY GOD. THAT REALLY IS TERRIFYING.

TERROR WAS REALLY THE ONLY TOOL THEY HAD LEFT. WHAT **WE** HAD TO DO WAS **REFUSE TO BE SCARED**.

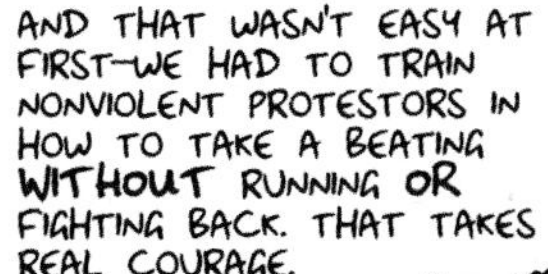

AND THAT WASN'T EASY AT FIRST—WE HAD TO TRAIN NONVIOLENT PROTESTORS IN HOW TO TAKE A BEATING **WITHOUT** RUNNING **OR** FIGHTING BACK. THAT TAKES REAL COURAGE.

BUT LOOK, IT WAS A START. ONE THING I REALLY NOTICED WAS THE POWER OF A NEW INVENTION THAT WAS SWEEPING AMERICA: **TELEVISION**!

TV MADE IT HARDER FOR THE REST OF AMERICA TO KEEP TURNING A BLIND EYE.

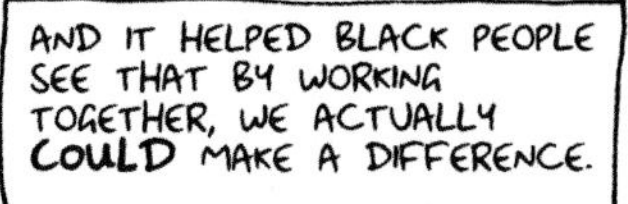

AND IT HELPED BLACK PEOPLE SEE THAT BY WORKING TOGETHER, WE ACTUALLY **COULD** MAKE A DIFFERENCE.

NONVIOLENT PROTESTS BEGAN SPRINGING UP ALL OVER THE PLACE, WITH THOUSANDS OF COURAGEOUS ACTIVISTS RISKING ARREST, INJURY, AND EVEN DEATH FOR WHAT THEY BELIEVED.

THEY HELD **SIT-INS** WHERE BLACK PROTESTORS WOULD SIT IN THE "WHITE ONLY" SECTIONS OF RESTAURANTS, PARKS, EVEN LIBRARIES...

THEY HELD **KNEEL-INS**, WHERE BLACK WORSHIPPERS JOINED WHITE-ONLY CHURCH SERVICES...

LET'S SEE HOW **CHRISTIAN** YOU ARE **NOW**...

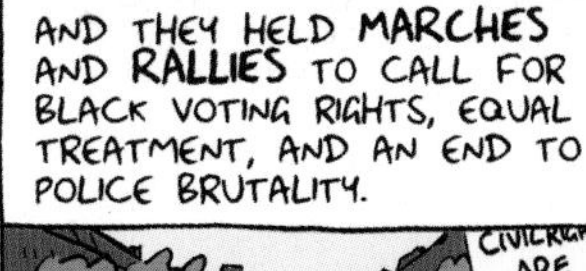

AND THEY HELD **MARCHES** AND **RALLIES** TO CALL FOR BLACK VOTING RIGHTS, EQUAL TREATMENT, AND AN END TO POLICE BRUTALITY.

END segregation NOW!
CIVIL RIGHTS ARE HUMAN RIGHTS

LOCAL GOVERNMENTS TRIED PASSING LAWS MAKING **ALL** FORMS OF PROTEST ILLEGAL, BUT WE CALLED THEIR BLUFF, CRAMMING THEIR JAILS TO **BURSTING**.

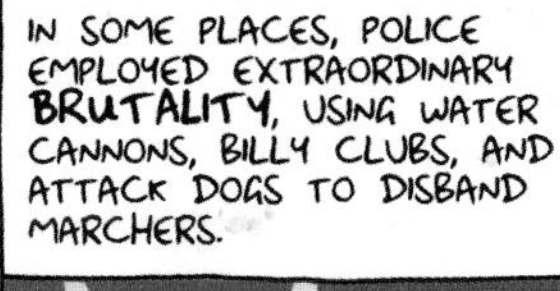

IN SOME PLACES, POLICE EMPLOYED EXTRAORDINARY **BRUTALITY**, USING WATER CANNONS, BILLY CLUBS, AND ATTACK DOGS TO DISBAND MARCHERS.

IT WAS HORRIFIC. BUT IT WAS **ALSO** ALL OVER THE NEWS. NOW **NO ONE** COULD IGNORE THE INJUSTICES **WE** LIVED EVERY DAY.

INSPIRED BY THE PROTESTORS' COURAGE, AND EMBARRASSED BY THE INTERNATIONAL OUTRAGE, PRESIDENT **JOHN F. KENNEDY** CALLED FOR CIVIL RIGHTS REFORMS.

ALONG WITH ALMOST A QUARTER OF A **MILLION** PROTESTORS, YOU MARCHED ON THE CAPITOL TO PUT YOUR DEMANDS TO THE PRESIDENT.

IT WAS THERE, IN FRONT OF THE LARGEST DEMONSTRATION IN U.S. HISTORY UP TO THAT POINT, YOU DELIVERED THE SPEECH OF A LIFETIME.

BLASTING THE HYPOCRISY OF RACIST OPPRESSION, WHILE ALSO PAINTING A MOVING PICTURE OF WHAT A COUNTRY **WITHOUT** RACISM MIGHT LOOK LIKE, YOUR **"I HAVE A DREAM"** SPEECH BECAME ONE OF THE MOST FAMOUS OF THE MODERN AGE.

I HAVE A DREAM
THAT MY FOUR LITTLE CHILDREN
WILL ONE DAY LIVE IN A NATION
WHERE THEY WILL NOT BE JUDGED
BY THE COLOR OF THEIR SKIN
BUT BY THE CONTENT OF THEIR CHARACTER.

IT WAS THE TURNING OF THE TIDE. OVER THE NEXT FEW YEARS, THE GOVERNMENT PASSED A SERIES OF RADICAL NEW LAWS, BANNING ALL FORMS OF SEGREGATION AND GUARANTEEING BLACK PEOPLES' RIGHT TO VOTE.

YOU WON THE **NOBEL PEACE PRIZE** FOR YOUR EFFORTS, AND WERE ALSO NAMED **TIME** MAGAZINE'S **MAN OF THE YEAR**.

TIME

AND WE EFFECTIVELY ENDED THE REIGN OF TERROR IN THE SOUTH. FACED WITH INCREASED SCRUTINY, STATE GOVERNMENTS STARTED CLAMPING DOWN ON DOMESTIC TERRORISTS.

WHAT IS THIS, MAN? I THOUGHT YOU WERE ON OUR SIDE!

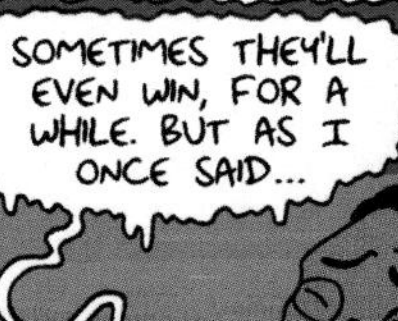

CORPSE TALK PRESENTS:
QUOTES from the KING
EXCLUSIVE
THE TIME IS ALWAYS RIPE TO DO RIGHT.
INJUSTICE ANYWHERE IS A THREAT TO JUSTICE EVERYWHERE.
DEALS
OUR SCIENTIFIC POWER HAS OUTRUN OUR SPIRITUAL POWER. WE HAVE GUIDED MISSILES AND MISGUIDED MEN.
OUR LIVES BEGIN TO END THE DAY WE BECOME SILENT ABOUT THINGS THAT MATTER.
WE MUST LEARN TO LIVE TOGETHER AS BROTHERS OR PERISH TOGETHER AS FOOLS.
SPECIAL $300

AND RADIO
DEALS
LET NO MAN PULL YOU SO LOW AS TO HATE HIM.
FREEDOM IS NEVER VOLUNTARILY GIVEN BY THE OPPRESSOR; IT MUST BE DEMANDED BY THE OPPRESSED.
THE SUREST WAY TO BE HAPPY IS TO SEEK HAPPINESS FOR OTHERS.
YOU DON'T HAVE TO SEE THE WHOLE STAIRCASE, JUST TAKE THE FIRST STEP.
YOU WILL CHANGE YOUR MIND; YOU WILL CHANGE YOUR LOOKS; YOU WILL CHANGE YOUR SMILE, LAUGH, AND WAYS, BUT NO MATTER WHAT YOU CHANGE, YOU WILL ALWAYS BE YOU.
I HAVE DECIDED TO STICK WITH LOVE. HATE IS TOO GREAT A BURDEN TO BEAR.

THAT WAS DEAD GOOD!
AND, TO THINK, EVERY ONE OF THESE RADICAL REBELS WAS JUST A REGULAR PERSON WHO REFUSED TO ACCEPT THAT THE WAY THINGS ARE IS THE BEST THEY CAN BE.
BUT WE'VE STILL ONLY SCRATCHED THE SURFACE OF ALL THE DEAD AMAZING PEOPLE FROM HISTORY...
PHEW! I'D BETTER GET DIGGING!

more CORPSE TALK available now!

CORPSE TALK
QUEENS & KINGS
AND OTHER ROYAL ROTTERS
Adam & Lisa Murphy

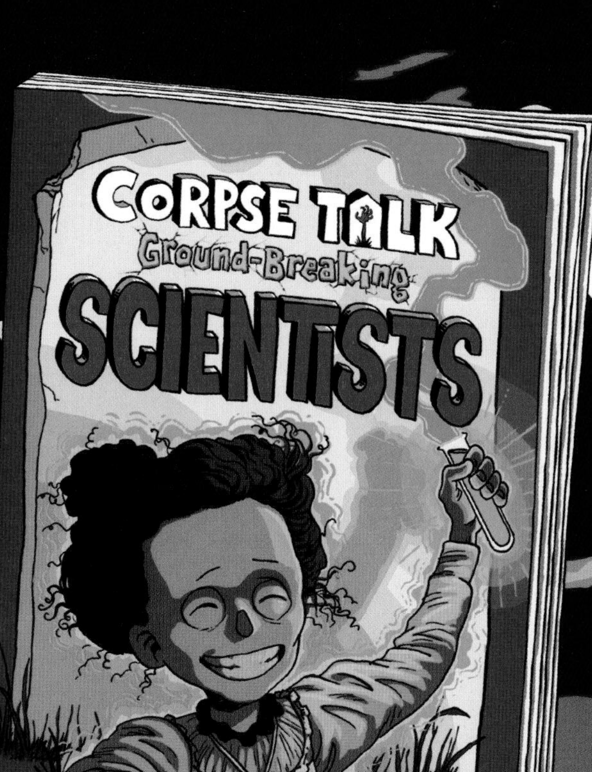
CORPSE TALK
Ground-Breaking
SCIENTISTS
Adam & Lisa Murphy

CORPSE TALK
Ground-Breaking
WOMEN
Adam & Lisa Murphy

Glossary

ARISTOCRACY CLASS OF PEOPLE WITH THE HIGHEST RANK AND PRIVILEGE IN SOCIETY.

ATHEISM BELIEF THAT THERE IS NO GOD.

BOYCOTT REFUSING TO TAKE PART IN SOMETHING, FOR EXAMPLE: AN ELECTION.

CATHOLIC A MEMBER OF THE CATHOLIC CHURCH—THE BRANCH OF THE CHRISTIAN RELIGION THAT ACCEPTS THE POPE AS ITS LEADER.

CIVIL WAR WAR BETWEEN PEOPLE OF THE SAME COUNTRY.

CONFISCATE TAKING AWAY A PERSON'S PROPERTY LEGALLY. DONE BY A HIGHER AUTHORITY FOR PURPOSES OF SAFETY OR PUNISHMENT.

DELEGATES PEOPLE CHOSEN OR ELECTED TO REPRESENT A LARGER GROUP, FOR EXAMPLE AT A CONFERENCE OR GOVERNMENT MEETING.

DICTATOR AN ABSOLUTE RULER WHOSE WORD IS LAW, USUALLY ONE WHO TOOK POWER BY FORCE.

EMPIRE A STATE FORMED BY ONE COUNTRY CONQUERING AND RULING A LOT OF DIFFERENT COUNTRIES, PEOPLES, OR LANDS.

THE ENLIGHTENMENT A MOVEMENT OF PHILOSOPHICAL THOUGHT AND IDEAS IN EUROPE DURING THE 17TH AND 18TH CENTURIES THAT EMPHASIZED THE IMPORTANCE OF RATIONAL THOUGHT.

EXCOMMUNICATION THE ACTION OF OFFICIALLY EXCLUDING SOMEONE FROM TAKING PART IN THE SACRAMENTS (RITES) AND SERVICES OF THE CHRISTIAN CHURCH.

GARRISON GROUP OF SOLDIERS WHO LIVE IN A TOWN OR BUILDING; CAN ALSO REFER TO THE TOWN OR BUILDING ITSELF.

INFRACTION BREAKING A LAW OR AGREEMENT.

INSURRECTION VIOLENT UPRISING AGAINST A GOVERNMENT OR OTHER AUTHORITY.

MERCENARIES SOLDIERS WHO FIGHT IN A WAR THAT OTHERWISE DOESN'T CONCERN THEM, PURELY TO MAKE MONEY.

PLANTATION LARGE FARM USED TO GROW CASH CROPS (CROPS SOLD FOR PROFIT RATHER THAN USED AS FOOD). IN THE PAST WERE OFTEN WORKED BY SLAVES.

PLUNDERING STEALING BY FORCE, USUALLY DURING A TIME OF WAR OR UNREST.

PROPAGANDA COMMUNICATION DESIGNED TO INFLUENCE HOW PEOPLE THINK AND BEHAVE—OFTEN MISLEADING OR FALSE.

PURGE TO GET RID OF PEOPLE OR THINGS CONSIDERED UNDESIRABLE OR IMPURE.

RANSOM SUM OF MONEY DEMANDED FOR THE RELEASE OF A PRISONER OR KIDNAPPED PERSON.

REINFORCEMENTS ADDITIONAL PEOPLE SENT TO INCREASE THE STRENGTH OF AN ARMY OR POLICE FORCE.

RESERVATIONS AREAS OF LAND "RESERVED" BY THE U.S. GOVERNMENT FOR NATIVE AMERICANS TO LIVE ON, AND MANAGED BY A SPECIFIC TRIBE OR NATION.

SEGREGATION THE ORGANIZED SEPARATION OF GROUPS OF PEOPLE IN DAILY LIFE, ON THE BASIS OF DIFFERENT RACE, RELIGION, ETC. (MAY INVOLVE DIFFERENT RESIDENTIAL AREAS, PUBLIC FACILITIES, GOVERNMENT INSTITUTIONS, LAWS, ETC.)

STOIC PERSON WHO CAN ENDURE HARDSHIP OR PAIN WITHOUT SHOWING THEIR FEELINGS OR COMPLAINING. NAMED AFTER AN ANCIENT GREEK PHILOSOPHY WHICH ENCOURAGED INNER CALM BY ACCEPTING YOUR PLACE IN THE NATURAL ORDER OF THE WORLD.

STRATEGIST PERSON SKILLED IN PLANNING ACTION OR POLICY, FOR EXAMPLE, IN WAR OR IN POLITICS.

SUPPRESS USE FORCE TO PUT AN END TO SOMETHING.

TERRORIST PERSON WHO USES VIOLENCE AND FEAR TO PROMOTE A PARTICULAR POLITICAL OR IDEOLOGICAL AIM.

TREASON THE CRIME OF BETRAYING ONE'S LEADER OR COUNTRY.

TYRANNY OPPRESSIVE, UNJUST, AND CRUEL USE OF POWER AND CONTROL BY A RULER OR GOVERNMENT.

VODOU RELIGION PRACTICED BY HAITIANS—A COMPLEX MIXTURE OF CATHOLIC CHRISTIANITY AND TRADITIONAL WEST AFRICAN RELIGIONS.

OK, I DON'T KNOW. HOW MANY SKELETONS DOES IT TAKE TO CHANGE A LIGHTBULB?

For Sophie, Finn, Ezra, Maisie, Teddy and Alice.
May you grow up strong and gentle.

Design and adaptation Paul Duffield
With special thanks to Tom Fickling,
Anthony Hinton, and Joe Brady
Senior Editors Marie Greenwood, Roohi Sehgal
US Senior Editor Shannon Beatty
Project Art Editor Kanika Kalra
DTP Designer Dheeraj Singh
Senior Production Editor Robert Dunn
Senior Production Controller Inderjit Bhullar
Managing Editors Monica Saigal, Laura Gilbert
Managing Art Editor Romi Chakraborty
Delhi Creative Heads Glenda Fernandes, Malavika Talukder
Publishing Manager Francesca Young
Deputy Art Director Mabel Chan
Publishing Director Sarah Larter

First American Edition, 2021
Published in the United States by DK Publishing
1450 Broadway, Suite 801, New York, NY 10018

DK, a Division of Penguin Random House LLC
21 22 23 24 25 10 9 8 7 6 5 4 3 2 1
001-322926-Aug/2021

Published in Great Britain by Dorling Kindersley Limited

A catalog record for this book
is available from the Library of Congress.
ISBN: 978-0-7440-3384-7 (Paperback)
ISBN: 978-0-7440-3385-4 (Hardback)

DK books are available at special discounts when purchased in bulk for sales promotions, premiums, fund-raising, or educational use.
For details, contact: DK Publishing Special Markets,
1450 Broadway, Suite 801, New York, NY 10018

SpecialSales@dk.com

Printed and bound in China

For the curious
www.dk.com

This book was made with Forest Stewardship Council™ certified paper– one small step in DK's commitment to a sustainable future. For more information go to www.dk.com/our-green-pledge